The I Peter 3

Girls

Sisterhood of Tragedy, Triumph,
and God's Amazing Grace.

Book cover design by Kim Kopec
Editing by Kelly Meldrum
Formatting by Chris Ott
ISBN 978-1-60013-049-6

ACKNOWLEDGMENTS

The publication of this book and the new Bible study edition would not have been possible without the invaluable support and help from very important people in my life.

As always, to my ever-patient husband Len, and understanding children, who put up with me during the most intense times with "the girls." Thank you for hanging in there with me in all the craziness that seems to follow me. I could not have done any of it without your love and support, I am so thankful we all lived to tell about it.

A special thanks to my daughter, Elizabeth. Being gifted and skilled in the field of publishing she passionately believes that we should do everything with excellence as Christians, down to our creative expression. Thanks Libeth for pushing for a new cover design. You were right!

The new edition would not be what it is without the encouragement, hard work, and just plain annoying persistence of key sisters-in-Christ who have pushed me and made sure this project is one of quality. Kelly Meldrum, I love you dearly and you really are nicer. Julie Wheaton, and Darci Ryke are my Proverbs 27:17 girls! You are in my face and have my back!

I owe a huge debt of gratitude to my Pastor, Rev. Brian Spencer, who, for 28 years, encouraged and discipled me, accepted me for who I am, and appreciated those gifts that others have found, at times, offensive. He has taught me much about erring on the side of grace.

To my "new" pastor and his wife, Tom and Connie Townsend, already true friends and family in Christ who have taken up the Hebrews 10:24 role in my life. Keep spurring me on!

To Nancy Dorner, who took me under her wing and taught me so much about writing, ministry, and most importantly, about prayer and obedience. Thank you for your inexhaustible encouragement, wisdom, and prayers.

To Sherry Rial, my heartfelt thanks for your friendship, encouragement, professional insights, and for letting me drag you into so many things.

To Kathie Dawn, because I said I would and I keep my promises.

Last but certainly not least; I can never adequately express my thanks and deep appreciation for my sisters in Christ whose lives inspired this work. You are my heroes.

GO TEAM JESUS!!

FORWARD

I cannot recommend Marlene's book too highly! As a counselor myself, I have read dozens of books on marriage and this is *absolutely unique.*

With marriage failure at 50-60%, every woman who wants to improve, strengthen, and/or save her marriage can do it by reading this book, then doing what it says.

Completely Scriptural, this book is a review of what God says about the marriage He blesses. Just believing in God is not enough to save your marriage. You must BELIEVE GOD and OBEY HIM!

Through her experiences of guiding and counseling The First Peter Three Girls, Marlene proves that God does save marriages even when husbands do not honor God's will!

Her knowledge of the scriptures, her own marriage building skills, her experience as a pastor's daughter, *and her believing faith,* have equipped Marlene to guide women into God honoring marriages and amazing answers to the prayers of those willing to believe and obey God.

Read this book, put it to work in your marriage, and expect to celebrate your fiftieth wedding anniversary in due time. God blesses those who honor Him, even if their husbands don't. Remember, with God *all things* are possible.

~Nancy Dorner, M.A., national speaker, author

TABLE OF CONTENTS

INTRODUCTION

Some say that there are worse things one can experience than death and, after reading the accounts of the women in this book, at first, some may be inclined to agree. But, within these pages, in the midst of the stories, is the heartbeat of hope—steady, strong, and vital.

The statistics within the church today on divorce and the devastation that sexual immorality is having on our homes and families are appalling. But even more disturbing is the response of believers to these unsettling statistics. Women everywhere seem to have a fatalistic complacency in their lives. They are buying the lie that relationships do not last and real healing is not possible. They are giving up on their marriages and, more importantly, they are giving up on God. Women in these situations have many resources in reach, but there are too few actual true to life success stories available to women at large that encourage and give hope that God truly does care about His children and works in their lives. In their darkest hours, The First Peter Three Girls craved examples of marriages restored through faith in Christ. By sharing their stories, their hope is to give other women in crisis a glimpse of God's light in seemingly hopeless circumstances.

My prayer is that women will find a consistent, prevailing thread throughout, proving that God is in control, that He never changes, that He still cares, and that He is all-powerful in our lives, even through seemingly impossible circumstances.

This is simply the true story of ordinary women with extraordinary stories of faith, struggle, pain, sisterhood, accountability, and God's sovereign grace that brought us all together to form what we have come to call ourselves, The First Peter Three Girls.

The I Peter 3 Girls

LORI

Some say that there are worse things than death…

I met Dan shortly after he graduated from high school. It was a new year and my husband Len and I had decided to work in volunteer youth ministry. We were going through our local Youth for Christ's associate staff training program. Dan was also in the training classes. He was shy but very likable, and being a newlywed with a mother-hen complex, I immediately "adopted" Dan. We were living in a basement apartment and eventually three friends, one of whom was our ministry supervisor at YFC, would occupy the upstairs of the home. Dan quickly became a regular fixture in our home and within our circle of friends. We had a lot of fun at the house back then with Bible studies, fellowships, and just hanging out, sometimes all night. We were young and immature but growing in our faith and sharing experiences.

It was obvious that Dan did not share a lot with us but we attributed this to his personality and shyness. He was just there, enjoying the company and, many times, chauffeuring the gang places since he was the only who had a cool car, a brand new yellow Chevette, a little cramped but what fun memories.

Over the next few years, Dan began to share a little more with Sherry or me at times, but only rarely. Thinking that he just needed to meet the "right girl," our goal for a time became to fix Dan up with a nice Christian girl to try to get him to come out of his shell. However, we had no apparent success in our early efforts.

The years seemed to pass quickly. Len and I moved and started a family and one by one the girls upstairs and the rest of our gang either went on to graduate from college or got married and we all moved on to the next phase in our lives. Dan went on to attend a university out of town, but kept in touch. When he was home, he would still come over and hang out or we would get together with some of the old gang, but he was becoming increasingly distant. I knew from talking with him that he had gotten out of the habit of attending church and was compromising on friendships at school, but I kept trying to encourage him in his walk with the Lord.

3

It eventually became evident that things were not going well for Dan spiritually. Doing poorly in school, he changed universities and moved back to the area. He was not in church at all and he began calling every month or so to confess his sins of partying and bad relationship choices. It broke my heart to talk to him. We would both end up in tears. It was like watching my own brother throwing his life away.

I am not sure what triggered what seemed to be a turnaround for Dan, but a while later he began attending church again and appeared to be getting his life back on track. We were thrilled. He was attending our church and becoming involved. At about the same time, one of Dan's co-workers set him up on a blind date. It turned out to be someone he knew who had gone to his high school. They began dating and he soon called to tell me about her.

My first question was, "Is she a Christian?" Without hesitation, he answered with a strong yes. I was relieved; things seemed to be rolling along for Dan down a positive, godly path. He told us that she was divorced and had two small children and had come to know the Lord after her first husband left her for another woman. I was curious and, of course, wanted to meet her. I did not have to wait long. It was only a couple of months later when Dan called, "I think I'm going to marry her."

I was stunned; he had gone from asking questions about Christians and divorce to buying an engagement ring inside of two months, all the while not sharing much at all about how he felt. I was curious now, but more than that, I was concerned for my friend. He called and wanted to bring her over so we set up a time to get together.

I really did not know what to expect since Dan had not given us much detail about Lori, but I was pleasantly surprised. She was pretty and friendly, but what struck me most was how boldly she talked about the Lord. She was a babe in Christ. She had only known the Lord for about a year and been divorced a little longer than that, but anyone could tell her conversion was genuine and her attitude was very open. At one point, when the men had left the room, she turned and looked me straight in the eye and said, "So, Dan says you know him better than anybody, can you tell me honestly if you think he is ready to make this commitment and can I trust him?"

That was a fair question after what she had already endured. This woman wanted to do what God wanted her to and her honesty and directness

4

humbled me. I answered her as best I could. I told her that from what I had seen in Dan's spiritual growth and what he had been through that if he was willing to make this commitment then yes, I felt he was ready and could be trusted.

As I look back on that moment now, I feel a certain amount of responsibility for some of what happened over the next several months and years. Now I exercise greater caution in answering those sort of questions. I feel that I failed Dan and Lori both by not spending critical time in prayer for my friends before answering Lori's question. At the same time, I know God is in control and Lori had prayed about their relationship and felt that God wanted her to marry Dan. Our human perspective is limited and finite at best. We make decisions based on snapshots in eternity, but God sees the big picture and already knows the outcome. That is where we learn to trust Him with our past and our present.

Lori had survived a very painful, traumatic divorce. Her first husband left her while she was pregnant for their second child, and, as a new Christian, she was looking for a godly man to be a father to her two very young children. Dan seemed to be a perfect fit, but we did not see the red flags and warning signals in Dan's life. The sad thing is that Dan considered Len and me his closest friends, and as it turned out, we did not even really know who Dan was.

Lori was expecting life with a Christian man to be, if not perfect, at least normal and different from being married to a non-Christian. Marriage to Dan was certainly different. She sensed something was not quite right even as early as their honeymoon, but could not put her finger on it. Lori and I developed a close discipleship relationship during the months since we met and we talked frequently. She was growing in her walk with the Lord but had increasing concerns about their marriage relationship. He was uncommunicative and distant and did not seem to want to participate in any type of intimacy. He was becoming more and more depressed and estranged. She, in turn, was beginning to question her own expectations of marriage and God's direction in her life, and she was becoming frustrated. It took two years, a series of difficult circumstances and stress, and the birth of their daughter, to bring Dan to the point of revealing what he had been hiding from everyone in his life for over 20 years.

On a Friday morning some two years after their marriage, Lori called me in tears. Dan had gone to work and left her a letter confessing for the first time what he had been struggling with most of his life. When I arrived at their home, Lori, still in tears, without a word, handed me the letter. As I read it my heart began to break and I was devastated. I had had no idea. I was stunned. It seemed Dan had been living a double life. In the letter, he informed Lori that he had been struggling with homosexuality since adolescence. The wording of the letter seemed to blame God and was hopelessly fatalistic. He could not change. He had tried. He was miserable and depressed and did not know what to do.

This was just the beginning of the long road God was asking Lori, Dan, Len, and me to travel together. It was also only the beginning of the confessions. We would soon learn that Dan also had an addiction to pornography. Dan had wrongly assumed that by getting married, putting on the façade of a "normal" life his sin would go away. He thought if he jumped through the hoops and looked and acted like a "normal" Christian then all the bondage, guilt, shame, and turmoil would simply disappear.

I believe there is no such thing as a "normal" Christian and that we cannot base our lives upon what today's religious society has deemed "normal." The standard has always been, and will always be, Jesus Christ alone. It is a much higher calling and standard than any outward form, habit, or tradition man has set. However, Satan is the father of lies and continued to lie and deceive Dan for six more years before he would understand God's grace, forgiveness, and the power to overcome sin that comes from the Holy Spirit. In the mean time, God would take Lori and I on a very intense and painful journey on which we learned about God's grace and forgiveness in our own lives as well.

The days and weeks following Dan's confession were an emotional roller coaster. We all wondered, "How do we respond? What do we say? How do we love and restore, yet stand firm on the very clear principles in God's Word regarding Dan's specific sins and how it had affected all of us?" It soon became apparent that Dan had confessed, but he had not taken any steps toward true repentance. At first, he seemed very relieved to have it out in the open, almost giddy. But it did not take long before he began to, once again, retreat emotionally, blame others, and manipulate those who loved him. He said what was expected and made attempts to participate in the relationship but then seemed to withdraw into a robot-type shell. He became very mechanical.

Lori tried to love and accept him as best she could and take steps to help him heal. She initiated conversation about their relationship, discussing goals she thought they both wanted for intimacy and communication. Dan would seem to agree without actually making any verbal commitments. She would do most of the talking, thinking that his passive acceptance was agreement. He asked what she wanted him to do and Lori made it easy for him, describing what she thought a godly husband and intimate marriage involved. Dan went through the motions of doing what Lori told him a good husband does in a very passive, mechanical manner. This lasted for a week or two and then he again retreated into a sullen, almost catatonic state. Lori tried to talk to him and draw him out of his shell but he became angry and twisted her words, and it ended up being "her fault." This cycle continued to repeat itself. Lori asked him questions, he lied and told her what he thought she wanted to hear until it blew up again and he confessed and told her what he had really done. He wounded her repeatedly and we were all frustrated and searching for a solution.

Lori went to our pastor and his wife for counsel and they advised them to go to a biblically sound counselor. Dan agreed to go to the counselor but, again, did not initiate his own recovery. He did what we asked of him, but did nothing without a push. Lori needed daily encouragement and struggled with her role in all of it. She wondered how she should respond to the situation; should she leave him? She also had to think about their children. They needed protection from this sin and the potential harm that could result.

What I respect the most about Lori is her desire to do what God wants, not just what seems right at the time. Even so early in her relationship with Christ, she did not turn tail and run, nor did she do anything rash out of panic. Instead, we began to pray for direction and for God's leading.

As Lori and I spent time together and tried to make sense of her devastating situation, we began to look at scripture to find answers in the midst of all the pain. I am privileged enough to have grown up in a pastor's home where the power of God was not only preached, but also lived. I knew what God could do and I knew there had to be answers for Lori and direction in the middle of chaos. I was convinced that God would give Lori strength and take her through the darkest days of her life patiently and lovingly, and sustain her by giving her sisters to lean on. He taught us both about the Body of Christ, about accountability, about faith, and trust in Christ, the One who loved us enough to die for us and suffered more than we could ever imagine.

Lori and I did not know it then, but our relationship was the first in setting the stage for the ministry that took place in the lives of nine women that God brought together that eventually became The First Peter Three Girls.

Pain, unbelievable emotional pain. Hopelessness and frustration. Helplessness and failure. Lori was feeling all of these things, and I was feeling them right along with her, along with the guilt of wondering if I could have done anything to prevent this or help Dan. Now, not just Dan's life was a mess, this affected Lori, three innocent, unsuspecting children, extended family, and even the church family. The implications were huge. Even though most of these other people did not know what was going on, it did affect them. In I Corinthians 5:6b Paul addresses moral sins in the church at Corinth, "Don't you know that a little yeast works through the whole batch of dough?"

Christians today are buying into Satan's lie that what we do in private is no one else's business, thinking, "I can handle this struggle. It is not hurting anyone else." These are lies and, in believing these lies, we forget the very character of God. He cannot even look upon sin of any kind. No one else may know our hearts, but God does. As our loving heavenly Father he must, because of His character, deal with sin in our lives. We are His children to love, grow, and discipline and when we resist Him, the discipline is painful.

Paul writes in Hebrews 12:6, "because the Lord disciplines those he loves, and he punishes everyone who he accepts as a son." Discipline is not always pleasant, and in Dan's life, it definitely worsened before he stopped resisting.

I knew by this time some of the choices Dan made during adolescence that started him on the path that got him to this point. Our pastor often says that each of us has full freedom over the choices we make, but we do not have freedom over the results of those choices. It was painfully clear that Dan walked this road because of his choices.

I wondered, "What about Lori? She has to address all the unanswered questions bombarding her spirit. Why her? She is a new believer. Why, now? She does not deserve this. These are not the consequences of her choices. Dan lied to her and deceived her. Doesn't she have a right to walk away, to just dump the baggage, and start over?"

Lori began receiving a lot of advice from other Christians who became aware of their situation. Looking for biblically based answers and direction, she approached several people for godly counsel. She received a myriad of advice. They told her everything from, "Get out now and protect yourself and the kids before it's too late."

To, "Become a 'fascinating woman' and then God will make Dan the man you want him to be."

Someone told her to, "Just initiate and be aggressive in the relationship if he will not do it,"

Another said, "This is such a huge sin problem that there is little hope of Dan ever really successfully dealing with it or of ever having a normal, intimate marriage so either get out now or accept it."

As the circle of people who knew grew in circumference, most shook their heads, tisk-tisked, and turned the other way. No one wanted to deal with this problem.

I became angry as I heard much of the so-called advice she was getting. I am no counselor, and do not have any easy answers, but I do know the Mighty Counselor and Prince of Peace who does have answers. Lori and I turned to Scripture to find out what the Word had to say. Now do not get me wrong, I believe strongly that there is a significant place for Christian counselors today, but many times we opt to go to a counselor before we consult God's Word, while often the answers, though not easy, are right there in front of us.

Both Lori and Dan were going to a Christian counselor together but, for the most part, the focus was to help Dan deal with his crisis and to try to help them both work on the marriage. Dan was getting a lot of attention and Lori was getting a lot of "advice." She was obviously having her own personal crisis and needed not only to seek godly counsel from a professional, but also someone to come alongside her daily and give her encouragement. She needed someone to help her to keep her eyes focused on Jesus and walk daily in the secure hand of God through the emotional land mines of the situation.

God's Word tells us that in the Body of Christ, God does not expect us to bear pain alone. Scripture teaches clearly that we are to love one another, bear one another's burdens, and weep with one another. We have a responsibility to each other in the Body of Christ to actually get involved and walk alongside each other. It seems that the church today no longer knows how to function as a body.

God's Word says that the eye cannot say to the hand, "I don't need you." Consequently, we cannot say to a brother or sister in Christ, "I feel bad about your pain, but it does not concern me and I do not know how to help you," and then just walk away. When a hammer hits a thumb, or a toe strikes a rock, the entire body reacts. The pain throbs all through the body to even the ends of the hair it seems. It might even cause a visible cringe, making the pain obvious to others. There is a reason why Christ used the picture of a physical body to describe how the Church is to function. We are to be relational, not traditional, or superficial. Christ was relational. He cared about people, not what they looked like or where they went to church or whether they sang in the choir or wore a suit or even how much money they made or where they worked. He wanted to heal their wounds and hurts and forgive their sins.

It also appears that in today's society, the Christians' view of God has shrunk dramatically. Just before the new millennium, I heard a man speak on a Focus on the Family radio broadcast regarding the Y2K bug. His observation was that Christians have more faith in science than in God. We are more likely to think God will fail than science and technology. With this mindset, we rob ourselves of the miracle of knowing the awesome Father God who created us.

So, as Lori and I searched the Scriptures for answers, Lori began to get a picture of who God really is and focus on that awesome God, the One who created all heaven and earth and each living thing. He is the One who parted the Red Sea, shut the mouths of the lions, came down and lived among us, and died and rose again to save us from our sins and an ultimate eternity in Hell. The questions Lori had to face were, "Is God really who He says He is? Is the Bible Truth? Is it relevant even in a situation as horrible as the one she found herself in?"

I remember asking Lori those questions day after day. I am sure she got sick of hearing it. No, I know she did. Still, it is important for every Christ follower to address these fundamental questions, because if He is not who He says He is, then as Paul said in 1 Corinthians 15, "your faith is futile." Cut your losses and get out now, which, unfortunately is the reaction most Christians seemed to have to Lori's situation.

Lori began to take God at His Word. We entered into an intense accountability and discipleship relationship. We did not make a conscious decision to do this; we both just understood. Lori, still in shock, needed to go over this repeatedly and needed to refocus daily on God and His Word. It was as if the earth beneath her was suddenly gone and she was hanging on for dear life to the only lifeline within her grasp.

We talked regularly on the phone, usually each morning after Dan left for work. We agreed to pray specifically about each day asking for direction for Lori. She needed prayer and encouragement every day to face the terrible reality of the situation and we both knew the Lord had placed us together in this; even so, this was no overnight fix-it situation. Even if Dan did a total turn around, it would take serious work to heal and repair their relationship. But Dan, having relieved the immediate pressure of guilt by confessing, stopped short of repentance. He was jumping through hoops again. He changed clothes outwardly, so to speak, but had not washed internally in the blood of Jesus by giving up the sin of his heart. Consequently, on the outside it appeared Dan was doing better. He was going to a counselor, still singing in the choir, and answering all of the pastor's and the counselor's questions with the "correct" responses. Only Lori knew that there was no deep change. What could she do when everyone around her thought everything was fine, but her husband was living a lie and she could not prove it?

Two pastors, three counselors, two accountability partners, two men's accountability groups, and approximately three years later, Dan and the marriage were still at square one. Dan was not ready to face his sin and surrender completely to God and no one could force him. No one can force another person to repentance; conviction is God's job.

Lori and I were learning and growing and came to some conclusions about Lori, her role, and her choices. During these initial years of struggle and frustration, Lori began to pray for God to show her what He wanted from her. She learned that He wanted her to put into practice Psalms 139:23-24, "Search me oh God, and know my heart; test me and know my anxious thoughts. See if there is any offensive way in me and lead me in the way everlasting."

Again, we questioned, "God, You're saying Lori needs to change after what she has been through? She is obviously innocent in all this!"

My husband likes to point out that according to God's Word no one is an innocent person. "There is none righteous, no not one" (Romans 3:10). We all are born in sin. So what did that mean for someone in Lori's situation?

First, Lori found that she needed to get her focus off Dan and onto God and what He wanted to do in her life. It is hard when we find ourselves in difficult situations not of our own making to understand what God really wants of us. On a daily basis, we prayed for God to show Lori what she needed to do, or not do, or what she needed to change. It was poignant when He began to show Lori patterns in her own life that may have been hindering God's work in Dan.

In my vast experience and studies, okay, not really, in my own life I have noticed that, as a woman, I have my own ideas of how best to be my husband's helpmate, and, of course, I let him know exactly what I think—on a regular basis, constantly. I must do this because apparently he cannot hear me the first time I speak and I can see things much clearer that he can. Well, Lori had the same problem.

Lori and I could see things so clearly where Dan was concerned. We would listen to the sermons and watch Dan out of the corner of our eyes, then ask each other, "How can he sit and listen to that and not see it?"

Time for a reality check—it was God's business how and when He would work on Dan, not ours. Boy, this was a hard concept to learn. We women seem to have difficulty letting go of the reins, and giving up control. We began to remind each other of this issue with a catch phrase, "It's a control issue."

Well, apparently it is always a control issue in our marriage roles, and with God. We would save ourselves much grief if we would just let God handle our spouses and quit trying to do His job. Lori and I began to get a clear picture that, even though Lori was not intending to, she was standing between Dan and God and she was a stumbling block that Dan was tripping over. Each time God would put Dan in a situation to deal with Him, Lori would jump in there and tell God, "Wait a minute; I think I can handle this." Dan's focus would then be on her instead of on the Lord. The more she tried to "fix it" for Dan the more he would use her as an excuse for his behavior. It was never good enough. She never tried hard enough. If she would only love him the "right" way so then he would be able to be a godly man, and on it went. She was getting beat up emotionally and it was her own fault.

It was difficult for Lori to grasp that Dan's repentance, or lack of it, was not her responsibility. She could not coerce his change, manipulate it, talk him into it, or talk to him rationally about it. She was getting more and more frustrated as he retreated into a shell of disinterest and passive-aggressive manipulation. She could not even get him to make simple decisions like, should they go out to dinner or if he wanted dinner at all. He was in his own fantasy world and

13

she was making all the decisions. Dan had abdicated his God-given leadership role and she had assumed it. After all somebody had to do it, right?

It was then that God directed us to the scripture verses in I Peter 3. Or, should I say, slapped us in the face with it. What a revelation! Such a simple passage and, actually, at first glance, rather irritating. We focused on the first four verses, "Wives in the same way be submissive to your husbands so that, if any of them do not believe the word, they may be won over without words by the behavior of their wives, when they see the purity and reverence of your lives. Your beauty should not come from outward adornment, such as braided hair and the wearing of gold jewelry and fine clothes. Instead, it should be that gentle and quiet spirit, which is of great worth in God's sight."

Our initial reaction, based on what society taught us, was to curl up our lips, repulsed by the images these verses conjure up. After God pointedly directed me to these verses and after I read them, it boiled down to two simple words I felt I had to share with Lori, "Shut up!" This would later become our simple creed to each other as women.

"If any of them (husbands) do not believe the word, they may be won over without words by the behavior of their wives." (I Peter 3:1b)

We questioned, "God can't mean that literally, can He? Are we really supposed to serve in silence?" It is a simple command, but it seems to be one of the most difficult for women to do.

We needed to re-group, re-boot, and re-evaluate. We had to go back to the bottom line again. Is God who He says He is and can the Bible be trusted?

Anyone who says that being a Christian is easy is lying or is floating down the river of denial. But anyone who thinks life without Christ is easier is a fool. Having a personal relationship with Jesus Christ is the only way to have peace in a situation like this and to have a sure hope that He can heal and do miracles. The secular world cannot give this hope. Our society would tell Lori and Dan that Dan was born this way and the only solution would be for Lori to divorce Dan and look for a heterosexual man, and for Dan to come out of the closet, give up his traditional family, and follow his "natural" sexual orientation. Just think of what would have happened to this family had Lori done this. It makes my toes curl every time I think of what might have been if we had given up on not only Dan, but on God and His power.

Did Lori get angry? Yes! Did she need to vent? Absolutely! Did she have to pretend that everything was great and put up a front at church and in front of friends and relatives? Absolutely not! As Christians God commands us in Scripture to reach for His standard in our lives. Lori had to figure out how to be real and honest without dishonoring Dan. Talk about a tall order. Of course, she failed regularly. But each time, with accountability, prayer, and support from other believers who knew God was in control, she would rally and trod on, step-by-step, day-by-day.

She would, if asked, admit they were having problems, but without disclosing the sensitive nature of the situation. She would ask for prayer for herself as well as for Dan. The church put them on the family needs prayer list, which, by the way, ticked Dan off. Because he was the one pretending, but she, with quiet dignity, would share discretely when God presented an opportunity. Our pastors knew the details, were supportive, and prayed fervently for them both.

Lori's dilemma highlights a misconception regarding the verses dealing with submission. Nowhere in scripture do I find verses that say submission is to excuse or cover up another's sin. It was not Lori's job to convict Dan, she needed to leave that to the Holy Spirit, but neither was she to cover up or enable his sin. Submission does not mean that if a husband asks his wife to be a party in his sin, that in obedience or submission, she should participate. It does mean however, that with honor and respect for his position as head of the home she decline gracefully and leave the responsibility for those choices in his lap.

Lori's counselor put it to her this way, "Dan has made a plate full of poisoned food. It smells and tastes awful. It will make him sick and it will eventually kill him if he eats it, but he wants you to eat it. He keeps putting it in front of you and telling you, 'Here, you eat this'." Her counselor told her she needed to put the plate back in front of Dan and tell him, "No, thanks, that is your food. You made it, you eat it." Again, that "shut up and let him take responsibility for his own life" concept. It is a command, from God, that seems impossible for most women, but it can save a marriage, and even a life, if we would just obey and, "shut up!"

Gradually, Lori began to take action. She was praying, reading the Word, seeing a sound biblical counselor, and in an accountability relationship to keep her thinking right and focused daily. She took steps and set boundaries to protect her children from exposure to his sin, and was learning to walk the walk of faith in a dark tunnel without any light ahead, just trusting the Father of Light to direct and protect her, and trusting Him to give her the grace to shut up. She had good days and lots of bad ones, but we trudged on together. Then, one day, I received another phone call.

MAGGIE

It was spring, approximately three years into my accountability relationship with Lori; I picked up the phone and was pleasantly surprised to hear my sister-in-law's voice. Maggie and I became friends over the nine years she and my husband's brother, Steven, had been married. We were not very close but we had a lot in common, marrying into the same family, and had shared some similar struggles as daughters-in-law. They had moved back to her hometown, out-of-state a few years before. We occasionally spoke on the phone and always enjoyed chatting. We did not have the opportunity to spend a lot of time together when they lived close, but we seemed to click as friends.

This time though, I was unprepared for what Maggie called to tell me. She was obviously upset as she told me, without preamble, that Steven was involved with another woman. She had found him at this woman's house a few nights before in the middle of the night when he had not come home. Again, the world tilted and things seemed to be falling apart. Yet again, both of them were professing born-again believers. I shook my head in disbelief, "How could this be happening?"

Steven is a very talented, charming man with a degree in music and a talent for writing music, directing, and playing various instruments. He was the music and choir director at a Baptist church in a small farming community where he and Maggie lived. The church was small, with only a handful of families, and they were thrilled to have a talented and charismatic man to help with their music ministry. He was the star.

Steven and Maggie's marriage had not been smooth sailing, even from the beginning. Maggie had only been a baby Christian of about a year when they married and he was a Baptist minister's son. Both with very strong personalities and a bent toward selfishness, they had not practiced biblical principles in their marriage, and in-law problems early on drove a wedge between them. Maggie, as a new believer and having come from a non-Christian home of hard working farmers, tried to deal with things the only way she knew how—she could handle it and no man was going to make her submit. She was tough and capable and did not have a clue as to what the Bible said regarding the role of a wife.

Steven, on the other hand, came from a very authoritarian Christian background and believed that it was a biblical principle that women were to submit regardless, no questions asked. He and his father, both, were quick to inform her of her "duty." He also did not seem to have an understanding of what his role was, as a servant leader. What was the result? She rebelled, and he became harsh and unloving. Sin is a vicious cycle that feeds on itself.

Not having a close relationship with her and most times only making small talk, I had no idea how bad things got over the years. She would occasionally mention her frustration with him and his irritating habits, but then would say, "I guess it's not as bad as so and so. So and so does this and I couldn't deal with that." She was always minimizing what was going on and ignoring the warning signs. Looking back, there had been definite red flags.

My heart sank listening to Maggie tell me where they ended up. He was involved with a woman at the church, someone who was going through marital problems as well. He was denying that he was doing anything wrong. He claimed he was not having an affair and that nothing was going on, and that Maggie did not know anything and that she was crazy. She had come to resent church, making up excuses not to go. He used any excuse possible to be there, even when there were no services. He had to practice music, all the time he would be gone, several evenings a week and all day Sunday. Everyone at church loved him; he was so talented and committed to them.

Maggie would be both relieved that he was out of the house, yet resentful that he was gone all of the time. As far as their intimate relationship, it was non-existent. He was sleeping on the couch.

She had suspected something for some time and when he had not come home that night, she tracked him down and found out he was at her house. She had sensed something about his relationship with this woman for some time and then, when confronted, he confirmed her worst fears.

Maggie's father owned a large farming operation where Steven worked days and had a very flexible schedule, while Maggie worked full time in the city. He had been coming home during the day and spending quite a bit of time on the phone with this woman, and then they began meeting secretly.

He eventually admitted to seeing this woman, but continued to insist that he was doing nothing wrong. After all, he had not slept with her so he had not had an affair, although he did admit to some physical involvement. They lived in the country, isolated to a certain extent, and Maggie had no one close to advise her, especially not at the church. She had no Christian friends close enough to call and, being a small church and community, gossip spread like wild fire. Those in the church who found out were simply shaking their heads. "You poor thing," and "He's in love with her, honey," as if there was nothing to do now. Things worsened and, out of desperation, not knowing where to turn; Maggie picked up the phone and called me.

My thoughts raced, "Now what? What am I supposed to tell her?" Knowing Steven as well as I did and his history with relationships, it did not look good. Apparently, this was not about sex; he was in love with this woman. How could she compete with that? Steven, having kept himself emotionally distant from his own wife for almost 10 years was feeling things he had not in a long time. He wanted to leave, he wanted to be with this woman, but his parents had drilled into him that divorce was not an option and he was struggling between his feelings and his upbringing. At this point, he was looking for a loophole in Scripture to get him out of his marriage.

As I listened to Maggie I prayed, "So, Lord, here we go again. Why me?"

"Obedience," was the quiet response.

"But Lord, I'm not a counselor. I don't have a degree; I am not qualified to deal with this."

But God didn't want me to give my opinion, or to tell these women what to do. He simply wanted me to use the spiritual gifts He had given me and point them to Scripture and His answers. He would use the foolish to confound the wise of the world, and He even wanted to use me. The seriousness of the situations and the responsibility of my assumed position of "counselor" often left me feeling humbled and frightened. As I walked these paths with these women, I learned more about who God is than I ever had before and God allowed me the privilege to be there when He performed miracles that even fellow believers said could not happen.

Only by God's grace and power would we get through this struggle together, "So Lord, what do I say?"

God said, "Tell her to shut up, I Peter 3."

FIRST PETER WHAT?

I could not help questioning, "What do You mean, shut up? Are You kidding? Not again, Lord. Not this time. Doesn't she need to tell him what he is doing? He obviously can't see what he's doing to their family. He doesn't know how much this is hurting Maggie, or what it's going to do to his children. Besides, it is just plain wrong. Sinful! Someone needs to tell him that and who better than his wife who is feeling it and can see it clearly. She is the injured party. She is the victim, right?"

Maggie and I read I Peter 3:1-4 together and tried to decide what it meant for her in this situation. Should she shut up completely? How in the world could she do that and live in the same house with a man who openly admitted he did not love her anymore?

It was time for Maggie to get her eyes off her husband and onto God. How was that going to help her? It does not change the situation, but when we get our eyes off our circumstances and other people and on Him, things start to happen. And it is usually not our circumstances that begin to change. Maggie had to learn what God wanted to teach her regardless of Steven's actions or reactions. The more we focus on sin, the more hopeless we become, but as we focus on God, our hope grows and our faith becomes stronger.

The God who is able to do more than we can even ask or think was asking her to get out of the way so He could work on Steven and, at the same time, He was asking her to trust Him with what He was teaching her about being a godly wife. That is a lofty goal for any woman. What a totally ridiculous thing to expect. After all, she is only human. How much is she supposed to put up with and let him get away with?

It always comes down to this—is God who He says He is or not? If the answer is yes, then why do we choose to do anything less than what He asks? Time and time again we must let go and let Him do his thing, "Ok God, it is time to take You at Your Word. This is where the rubber meets the road."

By this time, I was spending time daily with both Lori and Maggie. Still talking on the phone, Maggie out of state and Lori across town. I remember feeling literally consumed by prayer. To "pray continually" (1 Thessalonians 5:17) became a tangible reality in my life more than it had ever been. Both Lori and Maggie were also experiencing a prayer closet like never before. Neither of them had met or spoken with each other at this point but I had asked permission of each of them to share the other's story and they agreed. Somehow knowing that someone else was walking the same path at the same time was an encouragement. They both had to apply I Peter 3 to their lives and ask God what that meant for each of them on a daily basis.

For Lori it meant not initiating anything with Dan. She had been doing his job and trying to do hers, and then nagging him about why he could not see the mess all around him. She needed to fulfill her role, but distance herself from the relationship. God began to show her that she tended to enable those she loved and take responsibility for their actions, thinking that was her job. She had to struggle with giving up false guilt and recognize that true love was, at times, tough love.

I remember Lori asking me, "Aren't we supposed to have an intimate relationship in a godly marriage? Am I not supposed to share with Dan my feelings and needs?"

My answer was, "Are you married to a godly man right now?"

She answered, "No, obviously not."

"And how do you feel when you share your feelings with him and try to communicate?"

"Frustrated and hurt."

"Exactly."

These men were not walking with God and they chose sin. What makes us think if our husbands are rebelling against God that they will just sit down and listen to us and say, "Oh, I see what you are saying, you are right. I will just kneel right here to pray and take care of that."

We have to wake up, ladies! If our husbands will not listen to correction from God, why do we think they will tolerate it from us? Our criticism, no matter how merited, just perpetuates the sin cycle. We must learn to save the frustration and put it in God's hands. We must shut up and get out of the way. It always turns out best when we trust God, even if we cannot see the light at the end of the tunnel. Remember that God built the tunnel and He knows best when to turn that light on, the switch is in His hands. It also may require giving up what we think the ideal marriage relationship is and wait for God to give us His plan for our marriage.

There is a story about a little girl who went to the dime store one day with her mother. The little girl spotted some play jewelry and begged her mom for a string of plastic pearls. Her mother bought the pearls for her and she put them on, beaming with pride. She loved those plastic pearls. They were beautiful. She wore them day and night, to school and at play and after awhile they began to look a little rough and tattered. The paint began to peel off the beads and the string was dirty, but she did not see that. She just loved those pearls. Each night before bed, she would climb up onto her daddy's lap and snuggle in front of the fireplace. She felt very loved and secure in his arms.

One night, while sitting in his lap before bed her daddy asked her, "Honey, do you love me?"

"Oh yes, daddy. I love you very much."

He held out his hand and gently asked, "Will you give me your pearls?"

"Oh no, daddy. I can't take them off. I love my pearls. I'm a princess!" He hugged her and she got down and went off to bed.

The next evening she climbed up in his lap again to snuggle and again he asked, "Honey, do you love me?"

"You know I love you daddy. You're the best daddy ever."

"Will you give me your pearls?" He asked again.

She slowly shook her head; "I don't want to, daddy. They're the only ones I have." Again, she got down and went off to bed.

The next evening it was time for bed and the little girl was quiet as she climbed up into her daddy's lap. She knew what he was going to ask.

"Honey, do you love me?"

With downcast eyes, she simply nodded yes.

"Will you give me your pearls?"

She didn't answer but slowly reached up to take them off as a tear slipped down her face.

Her daddy took her prized possession; those dirty, ragged pearls, and threw them into the fire. Then as she clung to him sobbing, he reached into his pocket, pulled out a beautiful string of real pearls, and placed them around her neck.

It is the process of surrendering that is the most difficult for each of us, but God wants to give us the real thing. God's pearls are authentic and eternal and when He gives them to us, we kick ourselves for not giving up the old ones sooner.

For Maggie, as she and I worked through this together, it became quite comical.

At 9:00 a.m., the phone rang. It was Maggie. Without preamble, "Can you tell me why I'm doing this again?"

"Did Jesus hang on the cross and die for you?" I shot back.

"Ok, ok. But this sure is not fun."

"As I recall the Bible did not promise you fun."

Another call, "So, how long am I supposed to live with a man who hates me and loves another woman?"

Again, "Did Jesus die on a cross for you?"

"Alright, alright. I got the picture."

She wanted to know how long. However long it would take God to do a work in Maggie, not necessarily Steven. I believe we have to agree with God because of who He is, not for what He may or may not do for us now. "Though He slay me, yet I will serve Him" as the song goes. God has already paid the penalty for my sin and I will serve him in suffering, even to my death. God wants to teach us maturity not manipulation. He is not the big "sugar daddy" in the sky to give us whatever we want just because we are uncomfortable or in pain. He gives us His best, even if it hurts at first. If Steven never told Maggie he loved her again, what would be her response to God's command for her to be a godly wife?

During our conversations, which occurred several times a day, she would share her feelings and vent, which is normal and healthy. The response, however, always had to be, "Get your eyes off Steven and on God. What are you to do today? You can vent, but you cannot wallow in it."

The words of I Peter 3 became a daily discipline. We tried to come up with word pictures to help us both focus on what that meant. Maggie said that to her it was like a dog meeting its owner at the door—no words, no expectations, just quietly licking its owner's hand. I know some women will have a problem with this one but, hey, it got us through. Radio broadcasts such as "Family Life Today" with Dennis Rainey and "Focus on the Family" with James Dobson have aired many programs discussing the role of women and wives, so we listened, learned, and tried to have fun with it. We would laugh and say, "Be a dog, girlfriend," as in the role, not as a degrading personal description.

Later, some of the other women who came along would come up with, "get in a FOG," meaning, Focus on God. When we are there to encourage one another, even in the seemingly small things like a word or a phrase, it lightens the burden. A sense of humor goes a long way in helping to make the joy of the Lord a reality at times like this. Maggie needed to hand him his coffee and walk away. Serve him dinner and walk away. She needed a sense of humor to be able do this and not feel like she was losing her mind. Many people thought these girls had already gone over the edge just to stay in these situations.

At this point there was little need for any type of conversation beyond, "We need milk," or "Can you to pick up the kids?" Steven was hostile and harsh, and she needed to emotionally distance herself from him, yet still follow through on her role as godly wife, which, by the way, was a new concept for Maggie. Because it was new, this task kept her busy and focused much of the time. She had good days and many bad ones, but God was beginning to get her attention much in the same way He had gotten Lori's attention.

Maggie also realized that she could not blame the other woman either. Not that this woman was innocent before God for her actions, but Steven made his own choices and so had Maggie, and she realized that she had not been there for her husband and someone else had. She began to pray for both of them and, when we begin to pray in earnest for our enemies, God tends to take away the bitterness and give us a heart of forgiveness. Now do not get me wrong, there was still anger and hurt in the situation.

Sometimes when we were being silly, we would talk about doing ridiculous things like taking lawn fertilizer and spreading it in the shape of an "A" on her yard so when the grass came up it would be obvious. We never would do anything like that but, being human, sometimes it would alleviate some of the tension to joke around and laugh. It sounds vindictive, but it was never malicious and many times helped let off steam.

In the meantime, everyone in the small church had heard various versions of "the situation." The pastor and one of the elders attempted to reach out to Steven, but he rejected them and it was very uncomfortable for everyone concerned. Unfortunately, the leaders and church body did not pursue the issue and inadvertently added to the gossip by not dealing with the situation.

There was no discipline or accountability. Maggie felt as if she had no support, as they seemed to turn their backs, on not only her, but Steven also.

Steven began avoiding church leaders and eventually began to give up his responsibilities, while still maintaining a relationship with this woman. No one wanted to deal with the affair and the staff and congregation ignored the sin that was eating away at the church from the inside out.

Maggie drew clear boundaries in the relationship, and began to trust that God can and will work through obedience and silence. Those boundaries were important. They are important in all situations as they help define our roles. A godly boundary protected Maggie and helped her follow through on her responsibilities, as well as make it clear that Steven was responsible for his own choices and actions. This was not about being a doormat. We learned that being godly wives involves having a proactive attitude toward our roles. God does not call us to passive martyrdom. This role involves setting boundaries that help a woman stay within the responsibilities of her God-given role. As a woman recognizes this, she is able to get out of the way and let the Holy Spirit work on her husband—it is that I Peter 3 model again.

Not being one to put up a façade, Maggie challenged Steven to call his parents and tell them that they were having problems. She gave him the choice, if he would not, she would. She felt that they needed all the prayer and moral support they could get. He ended up calling them and sharing a slightly distorted version of what was going on, but at least they knew, and Maggie hoped they would add godly advice or at least prayer support.

It soon became apparent that things were happening with Steven. During the first few months after the situation had come to a head, Maggie worked on what it meant to "be a dog" and, as she began to get out of the way and focused on God, interesting things began to happen.

I find human behavior and the paths we allow sin to take us down in our lives fascinating. Every time I have been involved in a situation where a woman is coping with her husband's rebellion against God, his behavior has always followed the same pattern. The Bible clearly spells out the consequences of unrepentant sin, "Do not be deceived: God cannot be mocked. A man reaps what he sows." (Galatians 6:7).

This pattern applies to men and women. Regardless of the person, circumstances, background, or specific sin, the response seems to be the same.

When God exposes the sin, the initial reaction is denial, deceit, and blame shifting, "You don't know what you're talking about, there's nothing going on, I haven't done anything wrong." And on and on.

After that, comes irrational anger and accusations. We push our spouse's emotional buttons and reason, perhaps subconsciously, "If I can get him/her to react in anger and sin, then that justifies my sin, 'See how you are? That is why this will never work. You have never supported me. You've never been good to me'." The words "always" and "never" tend to come up often. Often, we resort to name calling or derogatory statements about family members just to get a negative response. We know best where our spouses are vulnerable and it is like cornering a wounded animal, we get vicious in our self-preservation. We will do anything to take the blame and focus off our sin and us.

Then we experience panic and paranoia. We feel we are losing control and cannot manipulate the situation. It is scary to face who we are in light of God's holiness. We forget about His love and forgiveness and continue to try to fix things without actually submitting to His authority in our lives. We begin making deals with God and try to appease those around us. We try jumping through hoops that we think will alleviate the guilt and condemnation, telling ourselves that the problem is external.

"It's not me. They don't understand. If I can just get them off my back this will go away."

Or, "It's my circumstances."

Maybe even, "I come from a dysfunctional family, it's their fault."

Once again, we need to see God's big picture in order to be able to get through these times. How can a woman obey I Peter 3, in the middle of all this chaos? When specific battles we are fighting distract us, we forget that God has already won the war. In order to survive we need to trust our Commander implicitly and follow Him and His orders in the midst of the battle. Not just to survive, but, ultimately, to live victorious, abundant, God-honoring lives. As our pastor likes to say, "We are not copers, we are conquerors." God has promised us this in His Word if we will only obey.

So what are God's commands in situations like these? First, we need to agree that God is who He says He is and His Word is Truth. In light of that, if we truly want to be obedient to God we must obey His Word even if it does not seem to make sense, especially in the secular world.

Nevertheless, we must be prepared. To follow the Commander means going off the beaten path and through the jungles of testing while fighting the battles of growth along the way. This will test our faith and resolve to the very core of our being. It means, if we truly surrender our will to the Great Commander, He will take us through conflict that will expose our deepest, darkest, fears and make us face them.

Psalms 139:23-24 says, "Search me, O God, and know my heart; test me and know my anxious thoughts. See if there be any offensive way in me, and lead me in the way everlasting."

WHO ME?

As I said before, human nature and sin follow the same patterns in our broken lives. This was apparent with Dan and Steven. They had different personalities and backgrounds, and seemingly, different sins, but the same results. Each went through the different phases, to one extent or another, avoiding responsibility for their choices.

Maggie sought out referrals for counseling on her own and found a biblically sound Christian counseling center and Steven agreed to go. They both liked their counselor; he had a very direct, confrontational style. They would each say what they thought the counselor wanted to hear during counseling and then go through the motions of carrying out any assignments asked of them. Often though, the hour-long drives to and from the sessions were filled with awkward silence or palpable tension and anger.

During the first few months, things settled into a sort of mundane pattern. Maggie struggled daily to shut up and follow through in her role as a wife and Steven remained distant and uncommunicative. There were times when Maggie had overwhelming feelings that Steven was still seeing the other woman. She called home in the middle of the day and the line was busy, or he dressed up and left the house without any explanation. At those times, when she just knew, she confronted Steven. Not ask or argue, but simply to say, "I know you have seen or talked to her, just so you know," and tell him that he was going to, at some point, have to make a choice. Usually, one way or another, her feelings were confirmed. It was as if the Holy Spirit was telling her when something happened. She did not need to know the details, nor did she try to pull them out of Steven. She just needed to let Steven know that he was not getting away with anything.

Of course, God knows our thoughts and the intent of our hearts, but when we are in rebellion, we think we are fooling everyone, including God. Maggie was drawing boundaries and learning about tough love. She told Steven that she was willing to work on the marriage and that she knew God could heal their relationship and that if he wanted to leave, it was his choice, but he was going to have to make it. No one can force another to do anything against his or her will. Besides, who would want someone to stay just because he felt forced, and not because he wanted to?

29

At times, when they had confrontations, it was rough. Steven would say terrible things to push her buttons and get her to react. If he could get her to sin, as I said before, it would justify his. The cycle for Steven continued— denial, deceit, blame shifting, paranoia, irrational anger, manipulation, and finally, going through the motions to appease others. And on it went.

The phone calls from Maggie continued too. "How long am I supposed to live like this?" And, "Tell me why I'm doing this again?"

It seemed as if nothing was happening. Day in and day out there was stress, frustration, and pain. There were days when Maggie could hardly concentrate at work with the crippling emotional pain she was feeling and the knowledge that Steven could be meeting with another woman at that very moment.

All the while, we prayed on a daily, almost constant, basis for her and Steven, and even for the other woman. We had to refocus daily, taking our eyes off Steven and the situation, and putting them back on Jesus and what He wanted for Maggie. She still had to take responsibility for her part in the mess in which they found themselves.

"What? Me apologize?"

"Have you been a godly wife all these years?"

"Well, no, but—"

"No buts. If you've done wrong then you need to take care of it, right?"

"But apologize to him? You have to be kidding! Look what he's doing."

"Maggie, what did Jesus do for you? We will pray about it. I know, with Christ, you can do this!"

Well, Maggie had admitted that she had not been a godly wife for the past 10 years and she had not done anything to take care of it. She knew she had not honored her husband, nor had she been submissive. Now she was ready to take responsibility for her sin. She would need to apologize to her husband, the very man who said he hated her and said he was in love with another woman. That was difficult enough, but God was not through with her yet.

Later, another afternoon and another phone call from Maggie. This time she was sobbing. Now, even in an emotional situation Maggie is not an emotional woman. She is not weepy by any sense of the word, but this day she was crying. I thought for sure that Steven had moved out. But no, this was not about Steven. God was dealing with Maggie.

"I'm mortified." She choked out.

"My most horrible, embarrassing secret is being told around town."

I could not imagine. Then she brokenly began to tell me what she had carefully kept hidden for years. She had a temper. "Don't we all?" I thought. But, I did not understand. She had a problem with abuse, spousal abuse. She would get angry and "go off" on Steven. She would lose control and beat on him, throw things, even go after him with a hoe or rake, screaming and yelling. He had only gotten physical in return in the last few months during this whole mess. He now had enough apparently, and he shared this secret outside their marriage—with the other woman no less—and now it was fodder for the local gossips at the beauty salon in town.

Maggie also confessed to an Internet relationship with someone. In her rebellious anger, she got involved in a chat room talking with a man on the Internet. He made her feel attractive and wanted, but when the man asked to meet her, she got scared and terminated the relationship. Steven had discovered her on the computer with this man during a chat session. It was not long after that Maggie had found out about Steven and the other woman.

Humiliation, embarrassment, and shame. Maggie was definitely broken, and she had no one to blame but herself. God peeled back the layers and exposed a sin that had festered into a cancerous tumor in Maggie's life. It was time to confess and repent.

The situation was getting more and more complicated. I thought, "Now what? How can we go on from here? He hates her and is in love with another woman. They both spent years verbally and emotionally abusing one another, and she had physically abused and emotionally emasculated Steven with her temper."

From a worldly perspective, the circumstances seemed impossible—just like Dan and Lori's situation. It was easy to imagine there was no hope, and it was all too far-gone, but this was a turning point for both Maggie and Lori in their growth. The question, "who me?" became the statement, "it's me Lord" and from where I sat, this is where things began to get exciting.

The I Peter 3 Girls

Confessing and repenting is a bitter pill to swallow but, oh, what cleansing medicine. The Great Physician began to truly cleanse and heal Maggie from that point on. She had begun the change as she daily gave over her will to the Heavenly Father, but now He had stripped away the sin and infection that had been poisoning her life. She began to develop a passion for God and His will for her life. It was not just going through steps to save her marriage, it was living for the God who saved her and gave His life for her. Changing to manipulate our circumstances or people is not genuine repentance. Whatever we do, we have to do out of obedience to Jesus Christ and for Him alone because He first loved us and died for us. Maggie and Lori had to do what God expected of them regardless of what their husbands decided to do, even if their husbands left them.

Moving her focus from Steven to herself began to make a noticeable difference in Maggie, even Steven noticed, but instead of seeing positive change, he accused her of trying to manipulate him. In his own sin, he refused to see what God was doing in Maggie's life. He had no trust in her because she destroyed that with her anger over the years.

Should she keep doing what God wanted her to? Even in the face of her husband's ridicule? Absolutely! She was not changing because her husband deserved it or for him at all. God had commanded her to submit and honor her husband as unto the Lord, whether Steven appreciated it and believed her or not. Later in I Peter, chapter three, the author talks about suffering for doing right.

Maggie apologized but Steven had not really heard her, but before God, Maggie had done the right thing and God began to bless her walk with Him. She began to get to know her Savior in a very personal and intimate way, something she had never experienced before. God became her portion, her all in all. When we "turn our eyes upon Jesus and look full in His wonderful face, the things of earth grow strangely dim in the light of His glory and grace."

We considered Job who, unlike Maggie and even Lori, did not contribute to his terrible circumstances, yet when he lost everything said "The LORD gave and the LORD has taken away; may the name of the LORD be praised." (Job 1:21b)

Talk about trust and faith. This was what God was trying to teach us. It was not about Steven or Dan, nor was it about marriage or personal happiness, or even adultery, pornography, or homosexuality. The lesson was about, will always be about, our awesome God and who He is. Do we really believe Him and want the kind of relationship with Him that He wants with us? Do we want to risk missing out on the only relationship that is truly eternal with the only One who will never fail or reject us, just for momentary comfort and fleeting happiness?

To most, it seems that choosing to trust God is lunacy. Even fellow believers who were aware of the situations would have the attitude that Job's wife and friends did, "curse God and die" (Job 2:9), there is no hope, why continue to suffer?

God's Word says to all of us, "I consider that our present sufferings are not worth comparing with the glory that will be revealed in us." (Romans 8:18). But I wonder, "Do we really believe this is true?"

Are we, as Christians today, even reading our Bibles? And if we are, do we actually believe what it says? Because as near as I can tell we sure are not living like we do. It was very discouraging for these women to hear the negative comments and focus of other believers who seemed only to see the human circumstances and the impossibility of the situations. Did they even know who God is?

Lori and Maggie began to see the need to distance themselves from those who would pull their attention away from Jesus. This meant emotional distance, even from their husbands. They still had to work daily at being godly wives, but they began to focus on God in earnest. God began to use the "it's me Lord" attitude in their lives to cultivate rich ground for growth and fruit in their lives.

Lori was recognizing her patterns of enabling and rescuing, and had begun to set firm boundaries and follow through. It angered and frustrated Dan that he could not get her to eat the food he placed in front of her. He continued to try to manipulate Lori, to get her to take responsibility for his actions or lack of them. It would take time for her to figure out how to set specific boundaries and how to respond.

Lori also had to deal with feelings of false guilt. She felt that somehow, in all this and even in her previous marriage, she was still to blame for others mistakes. She did indeed have to take responsibility for her own sin before God, but Lori had also spent years feeling guilty for things she had no control over. This was a huge issue for her and part of why she was always trying to fix things for everyone. If only she were "good enough" then maybe these things would not happen or people would not do the hurtful things they were doing.

Lori learned that the only person she could fix was herself, with the help of the Holy Spirit. This was actually a very freeing concept for her to realize. Lori found that submitting to God is a positive, proactive process, not the negative, passive one that most of us think. When we focus on God and what He wants us to do then we do not have time to worry about what others are or are not doing. It is just God and us. This thought process made it so much easier for Lori to let go of that guilt and get out of the way. Big things were happening with Lori, but it seemed Dan was still going nowhere.

Maggie, on the other hand, needed to recognize the patterns of anger and abuse in her life. It is interesting that once God brought her face to face with her sin and she was broken before Him, the bondage was also broken. She still needed to take a cold hard look at her life and make changes, but it was no longer impossible. Maggie began looking at verses dealing with anger and found biblically based articles on controlling anger from various sources. She was stunned to realize that she did not have to lose control, that even the act of losing control was her choice. We talked about the things that happened before she would go off and began to see how she and Steven would verbally push each other's emotional buttons. Again, it was about getting the big picture and recognizing what was happening. Once she realized this, she found it much easier to keep her cool with Steven. This began to change the dynamics of their relationship also. She was getting out of the way so God could deal with her husband, but regardless of what Steven decided to do, she was working on what God expected of her.

Both Maggie and Lori were changing, becoming First Peter three wives, and as they grew, their whole demeanor changed. The quiet and gentle spirit was showing through. Now, I believe that when the Bible speaks of a quiet and gentle spirit, it is not necessarily referring to personality. I believe it is an inner peace and quiet confidence that shines through no matter the circumstances, a calm assurance that comes from knowing we serve the One who is in control. It is noticeable maturity regardless of personality type. With it comes the realization that "I don't have to take control and I cannot change my husband, but I serve the God who can do anything and knows more about what is going on with my husband than I do. I can leave it in His almighty hands."

This is what was happening to Maggie and Lori. God blessed them with the ability to not panic, or bolt, or freak out when things appeared to be out of control. This strength from God allowed Maggie to stand, unemotional in the face of terrible, hurtful, verbal attacks and helped Lori to stand silent and firm when she was faced daily with criticism and passive manipulation, and neither having any intimacy whatsoever with their husbands.

It had now been four years for Lori and months for Maggie. How long did God expect them to stay in these situations? They had recognized their sin and made changes, surely God would relieve their emotional suffering now. He would not expect them to continue in these relationships when it was apparent that their husbands were not going to change, right?

Excuse me. Did Jesus die on the cross for us? Yes! Well, then, however long it takes to accomplish His will is how long it will take.

At this point Maggie and Lori still had not met or communicated with each other directly, but they continued to be aware of each other's situations. We eventually found a way to connect to each other and communicate together, but it was still some time before this took place. What we did not know is that we had just begun.

There is one thing that I found that Maggie, Lori, I, and any woman I spend time talking to, tends to struggle with. It is what I like to call what if-in'. What if-in' is a typical woman's response to any request that, in our perception, threatens our security.

"If I do this, what if he does that?"

"What if he never…"

"But what if I…"

We like to know the outcome before we risk anything. We all do it, but there comes a point when it is not simply apprehension, but it becomes unbelief and sin, and an obstacle in our growth with the Lord. We think we are questioning circumstances, covering our bases, making sure we have all the information we need to make a decision. It is how we are as women when it comes to our families and relationships. We want to protect our kids, our homes and marriages, and ourselves, but in some circumstances, we are actually questioning God's authority in our lives and doubting His love and sovereignty, "Does he really expect me to do this? But what if…?"

Lori had more of a problem with this than Maggie did. They both had to deal with what ifs, but Maggie tended to like a challenge and say to God, "Okay, what's the plan? Let's do it," whereas Lori became paralyzed by fear of doing the wrong thing. "But what if this doesn't work? What if he leaves? What if I say the wrong thing or draw the wrong boundary and it pushes him into the gay lifestyle?" The false guilt and lack of trust was just about killing her.

What ifs will totally immobilize us if we let them. That is where study of God's Word, prayer, and accountability are necessary. We need to get to know Jesus so intimately that we know what our role and responsibilities are so we do not second-guess God. We need to leave the "what ifs" up to Him and walk by faith, not by sight.

Lori had to realize that even if she did everything perfectly, Dan could still choose to leave. Once again, she could not act or react thinking that she could control or manipulate his response; he had to be responsible for his own choices. Yes, we can be obstacles to another if we are not walking where Jesus wants us to walk, but ultimately we each have a choice to make, and even if someone else is wrong, that does not excuse us. We must each discover what God wants out of us individually and then leave others' decisions to them and God.

Asking, "What if?" is blatant worry over things we have no control over. God's Word clearly tells us not to worry.

"But seek first his kingdom and his righteousness and all these things will be given to you as well. Therefore, do not worry about tomorrow, for tomorrow will worry about itself. Each day has enough trouble of its own. (Matthew 6:25)

Do not be anxious about anything, but in everything, by prayer and petition, with thanksgiving, present your requests to God and the peace of God, which transcends all understanding will guard your hearts and your minds in Christ Jesus." (Philippians 4:6-7)

According to God's Word, if it is serious enough to worry about, we need to pray and then leave it in God's hands. These verses are not just for good times, good marriages, or just the small trials in life. God means us to apply these verses in the overwhelming trials and humanly impossible circumstances in our lives. That is when they become real to us.

Is God who the Bible says He is? Satan wants nothing more than to paralyze us in our walk with God, rendering us useless to the Kingdom and cause of Christ, and in the process, rob us of the peace and joy that God gives us freely if we just believe Him and take Him at His word.

We need to face our circumstances honestly and place them before the throne of God, and then leave the worry to Him. We cannot afford to play mind games with ourselves and say, "It's not so bad," and avoid dealing with our situations and sin head on. Yet, we cannot afford to be so overcome by circumstance that we "what if" ourselves into a state of immobility, taking our eyes off God and off His power. I have often heard my pastor describe our lives as Christians as being on the straight and narrow path and that there is a ditch on either side of the road. Satan does not care which ditch he gets us in as long as we are not on the path God wants us to travel. Either way, either ditch, we become ineffective and distracted and end up missing out on where God wants to take us.

Maggie and Lori had to deal with the "what if" patterns in their lives. As they did, they found it was easier to trust God's direction. Still, we wondered what was next and where God would take Lori and Maggie. I would often tell them, "Fasten your seat belts; we're in for an exciting ride!" As the months went by this became more and more evident as the Holy Spirit did a work of grace in these women, but there seemed to be no apparent change in the hearts of their husbands. Trusting God became an extreme test of faith. For Maggie, autumn brought more darkness.

The I Peter 3 Girls

I Quit!

As imperfect humans, there are times in our lives when we seem to run out of steam. Even as Christians, we grow weary and faint and it becomes hard for us to just stand, let alone have the energy to move forward.

Maggie and Steven had spent months in counseling and then were told they did not need to come anymore. They had all the information they needed to make it work, they just needed to commit to do it and obey God's Word. But, their relationship at home had not changed. For months, Steven had been distant and at times polite, but made no move toward Maggie in any way. Maggie continued to work on her role as a wife and emotionally distance herself from Steven to be able to live out I Peter 3.

By autumn, things had started to deteriorate with Steven again. He stopped going to church altogether. Their roles had reversed. Remember, Maggie was the one who had not been attending church and she had resented Steven's involvement. Now Maggie felt she needed all the spiritual food she could digest and made it a priority to go. She had even followed through in water baptism, which, until that summer, she had argued she did not need to do to serve the Lord. God had really broken her and she was willing to do whatever He asked.

Steven began accusing her of going to church and talking to everyone about him. He became even more paranoid and defensive even when she had said nothing. He would say things like "You all think you know..." and, "You don't know me." And on it would go.

She could not go to any church activity without accusations or ugly confrontations. He was trying to push her buttons again. He was looking for an excuse, for justification for his choices. He thought it must be her fault, or the church's. Everyone was a hypocrite and we were all out to destroy him, everyone except this woman.

After months where it appeared he stopped seeing the other woman, someone spotted him in public with her. He fell again, this time harder. Maggie found notes and lyrics to songs he had written to her and to her parents. Was this ever going to end?

We continued to speak on the phone daily, sometimes several times a day. She was working full-time, trying to focus on her responsibilities, be a godly wife, and protect her young children from the situation, day in and day out, with no change.

She got to a point where she could not stand it. She knew she could not control Steven and confronted him with what she knew and told him he had a choice to make. At some point, he would have to leave and go to the other woman, or stay and work on the marriage, but he could not have both. She simply presented the choices. By this time, the strain was getting to her. She had to get out and take a break so she packed up the kids and left for the weekend, telling Steven she was going to his family. She came to our house to relax and regroup.

There are times when physical distance is necessary. She could not make the decision for Steven and she could not control what he would do if left alone. She needed to get alone with God and gain some strength to go on. She went home encouraged and rested.

The weekend apart had no effect on Steven. He continued to accuse, belittle, berate, and make irrational statements. As the Holy Spirit turned the heat up on him, he seemed to turn up the heat on Maggie.

The holidays were terrible; Christmas with the entire family was awkward. Maggie had the feeling that he had seen the other woman just before they left for our family Christmas. Steven remained distant with the family and avoided anything but superficial conversation.

When they returned home after the holidays, Steven began to get even angrier. Maggie wasn't sure what was going on or if she could continue to take it. I remember one day, around February, she called me in the morning from work.

"I'm over it. I am done. I quit. I want out." Her tone was cold and emotionless.

It scared me. I do not give in to tears easily, but I began to cry. I knew this was a turning point. It could go either way for her right then and the outcome scared me to death.

"Please don't give up. Please don't give up on God. Not now."

We had spent months talking about what God wanted in our lives. Asking, "Is He real? Does obedience matter? Can He do what the Bible says? Is the Bible truth? Did Jesus really die on the cross for us?" I had asked her the same questions dozens of times; going over it at this point would not matter. It was down to the wire. I do not even remember what I said or what her specific response was, I just know that at some point she chose God, whatever the cost. Each time God asked Maggie to submit to His Word and trust Him, as she surrendered to His will, there was a time of peace and growth. Each time He would give her direction and she would feel a confidence in acting on whatever He was leading her to do. The next area became dealing with the church issue.

It had been months since Steven had gone anywhere to church. He continued to accuse her of talking to everyone and spreading gossip each time she left the house to go. She asked me how she could remove this stumbling block for Steven and how she could get out of the way so he could not make false accusations.

We talked quite a bit about the situation. She was having a hard time dealing with the conflict every time she wanted to go to church. I said, "why not stay home for a while?" It might have been radical thinking, and it certainly did not make sense, but it would not be forever and we knew she would still be in a position of accountability and growing spiritually. She was not getting real biblical support from the small local body they had been attending, and the other woman's family was one of the longtime pillars and very involved in the church. Everyone seemed to want to ignore the situation and hope it would go away.

Maggie prayed about it and made the decision to stay home with Steven. His reaction was interesting. "Aren't you going to church?" he asked.

"No, not if you're not." She simply let him know that when he was ready to go back, she would gladly follow him to the church of his choice. This was a 180-degree change from the old Maggie. She would have never just followed her husband anywhere. God was changing her and Steven was noticing.

It did not mean that the pain and hurt were all gone nor did the circumstances change immediately, but Maggie truly began to give up control in everything to God. She was recognizing that God was peeling back the layers and each layer would bring new submission, and new trust in the God who loved her enough to die for her.

It would be a year later, almost two years from when everything had come to a head that the miraculous occurred.

The I Peter 3 Girls

HE LOVES ME NOT! HE LOVES ME!

I do not know how many times during that two-year period that Maggie repeatedly asked me "How long am I supposed to do this?" Again and again, I replied, "As long as God asks you to."

The last time that she remembered Steven telling her how he really felt about her was in a conversation they had dealing with his parents and their reaction to the situation. Maggie told Steven that she thought his mother hated her and his response was "I hated you long before my mother hated you."

There it was, he had said it aloud, and she had to deal with it. Not only was he in love with another woman, but he also hated Maggie. Did she really have to live in the same house with a man who openly hated her? She had lost her emotional security, humbled herself and admitted her sin to God, and apologized to Steven. She had given up church and her body of believers. There was strain on her relationship with her parents because they were not Christians and did not understand her decisions and reactions to the situation. She had no pride left. She had given up the right to kick him out or to leave, and she willingly made him coffee and did his laundry. Was she a doormat? Absolutely not! She had a plan—God's plan, and she had to continue to implement it in the face of the impossible.

When she grew weary or discouraged, I reminded her, "Get your focus on God and off Steven. In the two years of our intense accountability relationship, we repeated this mantra thousands of times, daily. Reading the Word daily and acting on it daily until it became as natural as breathing.

I kept assuring her that when God did the miraculous, her life would be different than it had ever been before, and her marriage would be better than it had ever been. Actually it already was. If God only changed her and Steven continued to be in rebellion, she was still different and even better having submitted to God's direction and authority. God makes beauty from ashes. We should never think otherwise.

The problem is that most women think they just want what they had before it all fell apart. They would rather not know the worst and continue to live in ignorant bliss. I find that one of the most difficult things to understand. Why would anyone want a relationship less than God's best? We would rather close our eyes and pretend than change. We are afraid of the unknown so we want the "honeymoon" experience again rather than growth and intimacy, but we are fools to settle for less than God's best.

I do not know about other couples, but I would not want to go back to the first few years of marriage for anything. God's plan for our marriage relationships gives us spiritual depth and intimacy that we can never know outside of His will. Now, after over 30 years of marriage, I can truly say it gets better each year. It is not always easy, but God always honors obedience and the rewards are most definitely worth the pain. Remember, "I consider that our present sufferings are not worth comparing with the glory that will be revealed in us." (Romans 8:18)

Before this crisis, Steven would occasionally tell Maggie he loved her. Nothing meaningful, just expected. After admitting he hated her, he said nothing. He wasn't pretending anymore, but it was painful for Maggie to know the truth. But remember, the truth sets us free. With God, we can deal with anything. I remember her asking often, "Will he ever love me again?"

I could not answer that; only God knew what was in Steven's heart and where He was taking Steven. I knew God is always faithful, but there was no guarantee that Steven would obey God. However, there is the guarantee that God would honor Maggie's obedience regardless of what Steven did, even if it meant Steven would choose to leave, God would be Maggie's portion, and that is better than any earthly blessing or human love.

It was a year later, the following February, that I received a phone call from Maggie early in the morning. She was obviously excited.

"Guess what?" She asked breathlessly.

"He said it, didn't he?" I was almost in tears. I knew he had told her he loved her.

"Yes, he said he loves me," she was thrilled, shocked, and overwhelmed. She had gotten into a comfortable pattern of following through with her role and emotionally distancing herself, not expecting anything from Steven because he was in God's hands. Trusting God and not looking for her own results, she had simply faced each day waiting on God, not Steven. Then boom—He blew her away. Somewhere in the middle of all this mess, God had been working on Steven and He did not even need to let Maggie in on the details. God is so good.

Why do we think we need to know how God is going to work on our spouses? We do not even know what God might be teaching them. I was at a women's conference with the First Peter Three Girls and heard Bishop Wellington Boone's wife speak. She used the word picture of a woman taking her car to the mechanic for repairs. What if the woman followed the mechanic into the garage and looking over his shoulder began to give him her opinion of what was wrong. "I think that thingy over there is loose and you might want to check this valve thing over here and…" on and on. The mechanic would most likely say, "Ma'am would you please go wait in the waiting area and let me do my job. I'll fix it and come and get you as soon as it's done."

We, as wives, need to get ourselves to God's waiting room and let the Master Mechanic work on our husbands. Trust me; He will let us know when He is done.

In all this excitement with Maggie, Lori was still plugging away, dealing with the daily grind as Maggie had. I was so excited about what was happening in Maggie's life and I shared the encouragement with Lori. But Lori's situation had been going on for years now with still no apparent change. It was time Maggie and Lori meet somehow. They needed each other's support and friendship, and Maggie had come up with the perfect solution: email.

They say that necessity is the mother of invention. Well, we did not invent email, but our long distance phone bills certainly created a necessity for something. Maggie's field is computers, and being the practical woman that she is, she began to look into the possibility of email for us to try to decrease our soaring long-distance bills. She found and installed a free email program on my computer and set it up, and then I did the same for Lori. I introduced them by computer and we began to communicate daily by email, Lori and Maggie getting to know each other personally, sharing their testimonies, struggles, and personal victories directly. It was a great idea. Our theme of course, was I Peter 3, and it was working.

In the coming months, God brought several more women into our lives and the First Peter Three Girls began to evolve into a vital ministry and lifeline for each of us.

Maggie, Lori, and I were on an emotional high for a while. Steven loved his wife again and was actively working on the marriage. Maggie did not ask when he quit seeing the other woman; she just knew it had happened. Because she trusted God with the details, she didn't need to know.

Steven's attitude had obviously changed, and during those months, he would often apologize. It was humble repentance and he was willing to be accountable. Were things perfect? No. They continued to work on healing wounds in the relationship, and God blessed them in ways to help the healing. A friend asked Steven to assist with the music at a different church. He began to attend there, alone at first. This was a big step since they had been out of church for almost a year. Then he asked Maggie if she and the girls would go along. Gradually, they began to attend regularly as a family. Now that they were back in a church with solid biblical preaching and getting to know new people, the healing continued.

It was an exciting time for Maggie, and for Lori and me, as we watched God do this miracle. We kept up our communication often on email, Maggie being a great source of encouragement for Lori, who was still struggling with her situation.

From the beginning of this saga, Maggie had looked for success stories. She wanted to hear from people who had obeyed Scripture and had seen God do miraculous things. She found that there was a lot of positive information, but not a lot of people sharing real life success stories. Books like *Boundaries* and *Love Must Be Tough* were a great help and encouragement in giving her direction, but she craved success stories. Especially during the darkest times, when people around her said there was no hope. She knew that God was faithful and she trusted His Word but wasn't there anyone who believed the same way and lived through this sort of thing? Was there anyone who wanted to share a testimony of God healing a broken marriage? Most of the Christians in her community, as I have said before, simply shook their heads and offered pity, not biblical answers or encouragement, and she did not have anyone close to her willing to invest in her life.

The Bible calls us to lift one another up, not tear each other down. Philippians 4 tells us not to worry, always pray, and to think on positive things, looking for God's best in a situation, not the world's failures. As Christians, we must remember that society's statistics are not God's statistics.

I remember Maggie telling God that she would use her story to help and encourage others. She knew what it was like to need to hear God's success stories. She just did not know how soon He would ask her to step out of her comfort zone to share hers.

It started with telling Lori over email. Then, it was not long before God brought other women into Maggie's life at work that began to share with her about their own personal struggles, opening a door for her to give her testimony.

I cannot overstate how far God brought Maggie. She is not a people person. She does not do crowds, nor does she feel comfortable getting too personal with people she does not know well. She likes a good get-together and enjoys group outings, but is intimidated to share personally in front of people. She relates best on a one-on-one level, and God surely began using her in that capacity at work.

God also gave Lori the opportunity to share with a few women going through similar struggles. Even though Lori was still in the midst of seemingly impossible circumstances, she had grown in her faith and, like Maggie, had a burden to share and encourage other women.

There are Christian men and women in lousy marriages, with pornography and adultery everywhere and, to us, it seemed they were coming out of the woodwork, in our community, in our work places, and, shockingly, in our own church. We discussed, "Are there any healthy, godly marriages anymore? Are most people in church pretending?" It sure felt that way after talking to woman after woman in similar situations. The scenarios were becoming all too familiar, similar problems and similar attitudes, with most ending in divorce. We wondered, "Where are the older women teaching the younger women how to be godly wives? Where are the older men teaching the younger men how to be godly husbands? Where are the Christ followers that want to obey God's Word and be His men and women no matter what the cost?"

The more I heard the angrier I became. I was not angry at the sin taking such a toll on the world, but at us, the Church, for allowing sin to take such a devastating toll on our own. God gives us everything we need to live godly lives, and we still allow Satan to ruin our witness to our communities and even to our own children. There are churches everywhere, open arms to help us up when we fall, and friends who want to keep us accountable. Not to mention the books, programs, and radio broadcasts offering sound biblical guidance that are available to us, and still we choose mediocrity.

It became blatantly obvious that biblical, First Peter three attitudes were sorely lacking among Christian women who felt helpless, defeated, and robbed of any joy in their relationships. Maybe the problem is we are flooded with great information and opportunities but in this age of technology, we have less and less personal, accountable, intimate relationships. It seems to all be superficial. We hear something we know applies to us, but we have no one to talk with about it, to help us sort it out, and then hold us accountable to apply it to our lives.

We are so busy we only have time for quick small talk as we pass by, meals on the go, voicemail, texting, and short emails. We have no time for the commitments of relationship—to invest ourselves in each other's lives and share burdens, cry or laugh together, challenge each other, hold one another accountable to the Word, and worst of all, no time for personal, intimate time with God in prayer. It is far too easy today to skim over relationships on our way to the next event, job, and church activity. Not to mention, that we can just click delete so we don't have to deal with anyone anymore.

Maggie and Lori told God to send them. We each committed to be there for each other and hold each other accountable to God's Word, even if it hurt, knowing the outcome would be God's blessing regardless of the circumstance. We were walking this journey together and in doing so God would give us sweet fellowship and strength, and grow us in areas we never expected. He would also begin to bring others into each of our lives that we would eventually add to our group. It was an awesome thing to watch God work as He brought each woman to us through unique situations.

The I Peter 3 Girls

Erica and Maggie had been friends since childhood. They attended high school and college together and Erica had been Maggie's maid of honor in her wedding. They kept in contact over the years and at one point Erica had even lived with Steven and Maggie for a time before they moved back home and before Erica got married. Maggie and Erica still spoke on the phone periodically and Maggie had shared about the problems she and Steven were having and kept her updated on how things were going so she could support them in prayer.

It was great for Maggie to be able to share with Erica about what God was doing in her marriage and Erica became excited about the First Peter three concept. Erica, although married to a Christian man, still struggled with her role and responsibilities in marriage. They did not have a critical situation at the time, just the mundane status quo that Erica wanted to overcome in her spiritual and personal life. She was eager to be a pro-active wife and mother, but struggled with feelings of failure and insecurity.

Maggie invited her to join us on email. Little did we know that some three years later, Erica would find herself in a situation where she very much needed the support and encouragement of the First Peter Three Girls.

At the same time, Lori had been getting to know another woman through the Mothers of Preschoolers (MOPS) ministry at our church. Lori was involved in MOPS because her youngest was still a preschooler, and Jeanie had two small children. Jeanie and her husband, Tim, had been coming to our church for a while, but neither Lori nor I knew her very well. Tim and Jeanie joined our Homebuilder's Sunday school class, and Lori and Jeanie began to establish a friendship. Jeanie began to hint to Lori that she and her husband were having problems. Although Lori's situation with Steven was a sensitive and intimate matter and she was very cautious about what she shared and with whom she shared it, she felt God was leading her to open up to Jeanie.

Jeanie eventually opened her broken heart to Lori and shared that her husband was addicted to pornography and that she found proof that he had had several adulterous relationships with women he met on the Internet. Jeanie's life was falling apart and she wondered if she should leave him or give him an ultimatum. She did not know what to do, but she wanted to save her family if possible and protect her children.

The gut-wrenching part for Jeanie was that her husband, Tim, had been the one to lead her to Christ before they were married. She respected his walk with the Lord and never expected to end up where she was now. She soon found out that someone exposed Tim to pornography as a young boy and he had struggled with the problem before he met her. She was not aware of this until after it affected their marriage. She was blind-sided, much like Lori. That feeling of helplessness encompassed her. She asked Lori if she could do anything to stop her family from falling apart and becoming another statistic or if she should dump the bum, and get on with her life.

Lori's response was to invite Jeanie to join us on email. Our group was growing and the women were hungry for real direction from God and a place they could go to share, vent, and work through the hurt and chaos in their lives.

I was overwhelmed, at times, by what was happening. Again, feeling like this was a huge issue in the church. I wondered, "How could this be?"

All around us, there are marriages falling apart and couples losing sight of whom God has called them to be. The divorce rate among "Christian" couples and the rest of society is the same. Do we have nothing to offer a hurting world? Where is the message of God's healing love and forgiveness? As a church, or even as individuals, what are we doing, or not doing, that is obviously hindering us from responding to such a great need?

The Bible teaches that we are to be as wise as serpents, yet as innocent as doves. If we do not recognize the danger signs, we will wander in a wilderness of pain and disillusionment. The problem today is that we have allowed society to infiltrate our churches and attitudes. It is so subtle we do not even know it is there. We have traded sharp, biblical wisdom for a jaded skepticism and our innocence for blind ignorance. We choose to involve ourselves in things that rob us of our spiritual edge and then we close our eyes and choose to ignore blatant sin in our lives and in our churches. We compromise God's Word and his statutes, and rationalize our sin.

Then, in order to maintain our rationalization of sin, we isolate ourselves from each other. We do not involve ourselves in the Body of Christ. Women and men are not risking personal involvement in teaching one another biblical principles on a one-on-one basis, and they are not holding each other accountable. It is too uncomfortable. We are too busy. It is none of our business. We have a million excuses to make us feel better about disobeying God in this area.

We live in the age of information and technology, where there is a wealth of good, biblically sound, material at our fingertips. There are books, radio broadcasts, conferences, and concerts, as well as our local church programs. Yet, with all this wealth of spiritual food, I see in my community and my own church, people who are starving in their spiritual lives. They are in the middle of an oasis and they are dying of thirst and do not even know it.

Any woman who uses cosmetics knows that a cabinet full of expensive make up and beauty tools is great, but if we do not apply any of them, they are useless. I could have cupboards filled with beauty supplies but what if, every time someone came to see me, I answered the door not having washed or combed my hair for days, or bathed or washed my face for days, or used any of the products I owned. Then I would invite them in and brag about my stockpile of expensive cosmetics and show them all my wondrous beauty aids, they would look at me, and I mean really look at me, and think I was absolutely out of my mind. Why would I do that? That is why application is crucial. We must apply Biblical principles for them to work. Why don't we apply them? Pick one; "It is too much work, I'm busy with other things, I'll do it later, I just can't, it's too hard." The excuses are limitless.

Marriages take a devastating path if we do not apply biblical principles and maintain our relationships. Dennis Rainey published a book years ago entitled "Staying Close" that addresses the natural drift toward isolation in marriage. Every marriage, if left unattended, goes down this path. Once headed that way, we are unprotected and open to Satan's attacks. Unprepared, we find ourselves in an unknown, dangerous place, not knowing where to turn or what to do.

We do not check our compass, the Bible, frequently enough or we take our eyes off our Guide, the Lord, and we end up alone and scared. Lost and in a panic, we make wrong decisions driven by emotion, because we don't have established, intimate relationships within the Body of Christ so there is no accountability in applying the biblical principles that will get us back on track. It becomes too easy to just wander in the wilderness and let life happen instead of having a map and making biblical choices to battle our way back to the straight and narrow, heading in the right direction.

The First Peter three group was becoming a place to take refuge. A rest area of sorts to regroup and look at the map once again, get our bearings, and then head out together in this struggle to find our way back to God's straight and narrow as women.

Jeanie needed the kind of encouragement Lori, living it right along with her, could give her. She needed the hope that Maggie, having made it through to the other side of the tunnel, could give her. Erica could learn and grow by walking this path with us, learning the obstacles to avoid and becoming much more aware and wise in her own relationship with her husband. It later came to the point in Erica's life that she, also, began to recognize red flags where her husband was concerned and find that part of the reason for the spiritual apathy in their lives was due to a hidden addiction to pornography. Her husband, Tom, had struggled for years with this and she had no idea. Pornography entered Tom's life at a very young age, about fourth grade, and it had taken its toll on him and noticeably affected their marriage. Jeanie and Erica had similar stories, just at different times in the journey together. God, in His infinite wisdom, knew what we would need and when, and choreographed our lives to bring us together at just the right time.

I would spend my time with them going over Scripture after Scripture, and we would pray for direction for each of us to apply to our own lives and marriages. Their choices and faith would strengthen my own faith and resolve to be a godly woman and a First Peter three wife.

Soon there would be two more joining Lori, Maggie, Erica, Jeanie, and me on this journey. God added so much more to our group by bringing us different perspectives and spiritual gifts to encourage one another and, through His Word, He continued to bind us together in a way that transcended ordinary human relationships.

Life with God is an adventure and sometimes His surprises make me smile with joy.

The way things began to snowball with the First Peter Three Girls was definitely exciting, but watching the girls grow and reach out to others was the most rewarding aspect for me. If someone would have told Maggie a year before that not only would she have a restored and healing marriage, but that she would willingly step out of her comfort zone and share with other women at her work place, she would have flat out said they were crazy. Ok, I did tell her that, and I loved being able to say, "I told you so." It was so much fun to watch God at work in her life.

Maggie called me all excited that she spent with Mandy, a girl at her work, and had the opportunity to share her testimony of what God did in her marriage. One thing led to another, and as they talked, Maggie learned that Mandy had grown up with some exposure to church, but did not accept Christ's gift of salvation. She also learned that Mandy was engaged to a young man named Bill who was also not a Christian. They were living together and were planning to marry in the next few months.

Maggie and Mandy talked daily, and as their friendship grew, Maggie invited them to visit their church. Mandy was young, about 24 years old, and very eager to learn about the God that performed such miracles in Maggie's life. After attending a service with Steven and Maggie, one of the pastors visited Mandy and Bill at home later in the week, and they both made a decision to accept God's gift of forgiveness and salvation. We were all ecstatic. Maggie shared with the First Peter Three Girls after she began talking with Mandy, and we had been praying for Mandy and Bill for weeks. Mandy was hungry for more, and she wanted to join the group. We thought there was no better time to learn about being a godly wife than before walking down the aisle.

She and Bill attended a Family Life Marriage Conference, and as a result made a commitment to purity and to stay away from each other physically until their wedding, which was a huge step since they had been living together for a couple of years. They received a purity contract at the conference that they signed and kept. Mandy asked the First Peter Three Girls to hold her accountable to that commitment. It was so exciting to be a part of their spiritual growth.

Also, during this time Maggie was getting to know another woman at work, Julia. As they began to get better acquainted, Julia shared that her husband, Kent, had been invited to a Promise Keepers conference a couple of years before and had come home excited and shared with her his new-found faith and relationship with Jesus Christ. Because of his sharing with her, Julia also accepted God's gift of salvation. They were learning and growing in their walk with the Lord and, as a new believer, she was interested in becoming involved in the First Peter three group. Julia became, and still is, our cheerleader. She always has a positive word of encouragement and an "amen" when needed.

As our relationships developed, some of our husbands began to see the spiritual benefits in the lives of their wives and, in turn, in their own lives as well, which resulted in them taking an active, positive supportive role with the group. Kent and my husband, Len, were great resources for us for prayer, leadership, and biblical advice from a man's perspective, when needed. Kent is a wonderful, godly man, who has taken his spiritual leadership role very seriously in marriage and together, he and Julia have become our prayer warriors. As for my husband, Len, I will share more about him later on, but I am thankful for a godly husband who also believes God's Word and acts on it.

Mandy and Julia were an exciting addition to our group. Julia, with her quiet grace and encouragement, and Mandy, with her infectious spirit and humor, added a new dynamic. Mandy had just begun to walk the path of a godly woman and would have some serious struggles with her own spiritual growth and in her relationship with Bill after their marriage. But with God's direction and the encouragement of the First Peter Three Girls, she learned some basic biblical principles that eventually became a reality in her life and were the foundation for real growth and change later on.

Our little group was not so little anymore and God was getting ready to add two more women during this time.

Renee and Brian were our neighbors. I remember when they moved in several years before and their dog had gotten loose. Brian came over to get him and we chatted for a few moments, getting acquainted. As we talked, I mentioned our church and extended an open invitation. Brian immediately suggested that I not say anything to his wife, Renee, about church. It seemed an experience in her teens left her deeply hurt when the church she and her sister attended had split. As a teenager, not having come from a Christian home, and looking for the love and acceptance she had been told God offered, she became very disillusioned by the hypocrisy she witnessed and bitterly turned her back on the church, feeling she could worship God alone. She did not need so-called Christians.

Renee had been through a lot in the 20 years since that time. This was the second marriage for both Brian and Renee. Her first marriage, to an alcoholic, ended in divorce when he became abusive. Raising two small children alone, she joined the Air National Guard to support her family and there, met Brian. Having just gone through a divorce himself and with one young son, the two of them shared common experiences and pain. They married, and shortly after, moved into our neighborhood.

When Brian advised me not to broach the subject of church or God with Renee, I took that as a challenge. I wanted to show this woman God's love and that we are not all perfect, but that God does use Christians in the Body and He does forgive and heal.

When I did finally meet Renee, we hit it off right away. We spent hours talking about life and she shared what she had been through. I was amazed at how strong this woman was, but I knew that she needed God's healing touch. Through our friendship, she and her children began attending church with us, and she rededicated her life to Christ.

Then things began to fall apart. Brian had some exposure to church and Christianity and said he made a profession of faith as a young boy, but had not been in church in years and did not seem interested in spiritual things. There was strain in their marriage almost from the beginning. Even only being married a short time, they both came into it with a lot of baggage and hurt, and it was affecting their relationship.

59

When a woman has been through what Renee had, she tends to crave love and security. Security then becomes a control issue. If I can control the other person or the situation, I won't be hurt again. The more we try to control, the more we lose control. The more the other person withdraws, the more insecure we get. A vicious cycle was beginning to repeat itself in their lives.

Renee discovered Brian was seeing another woman and again I found myself in an all too familiar situation, asking, "Now what?" Did the same principle apply for Renee that did for Maggie, Lori, and Jeanie? Of course, but it did not make it any easier. Renee had some First Peter three issues to deal with just like the rest of us. It was time to shut up.

The "without a word" issue was the reoccurring theme in each of our lives. Why is it so hard for us to give up control, shut our mouths, and to take God at His word and just do it?

"The wise woman builds her house, but with her own hands the foolish one tears hers down." (Proverbs 14:1)

As women, we use our foolish tongues as tools to tear down our own houses and we do not even realize it. We criticize, ridicule, and emasculate our husbands with our words, and then wonder why they refuse to take the leadership role in marriage and why they don't love us the way they should. We use our tongues to stand between God and our husbands and become the blocks they trip over. Then, we continue to kick them while they are down.

Well, as with the rest of us, Renee had to deal with this area in her life. She needed to recognize her own patterns and turn them over to God, and then begin to change. Not to change the circumstances, but to become who God wanted her to be regardless of the outcome.

We had been friends for a couple of years at this point. Renee became friends with Lori through church and knew about Maggie and our First Peter three group, but only recently was able to join us online. It became a great encouragement to her to know there were other women out there supporting her biblical choices and praying for her and for each other. Brian did come to a point where he chose to stay in the marriage, and has participated in church to some extent, but has not committed his life to Christ wholeheartedly. We continue to pray for him, but Renee has a gift for communicating clearly and, even being in a difficult situation herself, her insights have been very discerning. So, adding Renee to our band of merry women, we continued to grow.

Another day brought another phone call. This time from a long-time childhood friend, I had not heard from in a few years. Stacy and I grew up together in church. My father was her pastor, and she and her sister were my close friends. As adults, Len and I spent time together with Stacy and her husband, Greg, early in our marriage relationships, but they started a family before we did and then moved to a small community out of town and we didn't see much of them. We still had a great time when we got together, but we moved on to different stages in our lives over the years.

This particular day, Stacy saw someone we grew up with, thought of me, and decided to call. It was fun catching up and we made plans to get together. We saw each other a couple of times over the ensuing months, getting to know their children, Jill, now 19 and Dave, 16 and enjoying the fellowship.

I always respected Stacy and Greg's marriage and their commitment to the Lord and His Word. I still did. They raised their children in a loving, Christian home. They had gone to the Family Life seminars, heard Josh McDowell speak, and bought all the right books on Christian parenting and marriage. They lived a godly example of marriage in front of their children. They were not perfect, but they were definitely committed to God's will in their family.

Shortly after we started to spend time with them again, Stacy called me crying. She was devastated. Jill, their daughter, moved out without warning and cut off communication with her parents. For several weeks, she had been acting different and seemed to become a very different person before their eyes. Then, arriving home from church on a Sunday afternoon, they found her things gone. She had moved out. They did not know where to find her or how to contact her. They were frantic with worry. This was not at all like the Jill they knew. When they finally did locate her, she was not herself. It was a cruel joke. This Jill was living in a less than desirable atmosphere. Rumors were that she was drinking, smoking, partying, and even doing drugs. She didn't bother denying it, but she did begin a pattern of lying about things. She walked out on her job and college. She avoided talking with them at all and she had her friends lie to them about where she was.

Stacy was beside herself with grief and worry. How could this happen? She called Jill's friends and tried to talk to them about what was going on. She tracked Jill down and tried to talk to her, asking her why and begging Jill to tell her what had happened. The more she tried the more distant and elusive Jill became. She wanted nothing more to do with church, God, or her family. It was mind-boggling. What was a mother to do?

Listening to Stacy share her heartbrokenness I began to wonder if the First Peter three concept applied in this situation. Stacy surely could use the encouragement and support of other wives and mothers. I invited her to join us. It is amazing to me how universal God's principles are. Jill was doing the same thing as Dan, Steven and the other husband's in crisis in running from God, and Stacy needed to let go and give her daughter to Him. She could no longer be a mother to her daughter. Jill was an adult and making choices on her own. Stacy could not control Jill or the circumstances. For a mother, letting go, especially in a situation like this, is the hardest thing to do, but she needed to shut up, get on her knees, and let God take over.

So, she too became a First Peter Three Girl. It was amazing how similar the emotional pain was to those women dealing with marital issues. We had a lot in common. All women, wanting to be who God called us to be, fighting spiritual battles and dealing with our own human frailties. What a combination of women and, together, what a powerful force in the spiritual battles God called us to fight.

Before I share what eventually happened in Lori's life, I want to introduce the most recent member of the original First Peter Three Girls group, Traci.

It was my daughter's twelfth birthday and we were taking her to a Grover Levy concert at a local Bible conference center. There were hundreds of teens and adults everywhere, getting their seats and talking with friends. I turned around in my seat looking over the auditorium for people I knew, and there was Traci, walking directly toward me. I had not seen her in more than 15 years. We had been best friends in Jr. High, but then in high school we went in different directions. She began making choices that led her away from church and God, and we eventually became like distant acquaintances.

After we graduated, she married Kyle, a non-Christian guy we had gone to school with, and after he joined the military, eventually they moved away. I had seen her only briefly, once or twice in the first couple of years before they left the states for Germany. I had also married after graduation, but Traci and I didn't seem to have much in common.

I remember one time talking with her about the Lord and I will never forget when she said, almost with regret, "I wish I could be like you." It was a humbling statement that I wasn't comfortable with, and I did not understand then that Traci struggled with understanding God's grace and forgiveness in her life and would continue to for years to come. I occasionally saw her mother and asked how she was doing and, in recent years, had heard that they moved back to the states and she had gotten back into church.

Then several years later, here she was, walking straight toward me. I was so excited to see her. She and her sister sat next to us and we tried to catch up before the concert began. We talked about our upcoming high school class reunion, and I asked if she and Kyle would be attending. She seemed rather uncomfortable at first, and then she told me that Kyle had left her just three weeks before. She had gone to a Christian women's conference and, upon returning, found he had moved out without explanation.

It saddened me to hear another tragic story, but it was another open door for God to work and use the First Peter Three Girls. Of course, I shared with her a little about the group and found she was looking for a part-time job. I was working as a lunchroom supervisor at a local junior high and knew they were in need of another person to join the team, so I gave her the information. The next Monday she showed up and went to work. We were able to get reacquainted working together every day, and she shared more details about her life and marriage. It began to sound terribly familiar.

Traci is a shy person and was hesitant about joining a group of women and sharing her personal struggles with strangers, but she did eventually join us, and as each woman shared her own story, Traci began to understand that she was not alone. It took her the better part of a year to really to open up and be honest about her feelings and what God was doing in her life, but it was an exciting time for us as a group. Traci joined us just after things started to get interesting in Lori's life again. Well over seven years after Dan had confessed his secret, Lori was still plugging away, being a First Peter three wife living with a husband who was living a lie, when things began to intensify in their home.

Seven years had passed since we learned Dan's devastating secret. For seven years, Lori had been living with pain, frustration, and disillusionment, but she had been living with something else too, hope. Her faith in the Lord had grown tremendously. She was able to counsel and share with women in similar situations, encouraging them in their relationship with the Lord even though she lived daily with a humanly unbearable situation. It was a powerful message.

Lori did a lot of changing in those seven years. She learned to set boundaries and not eat that plate of food that Dan sat before her daily. She began to learn how to recognize the false guilt and how not to let it control her. She was learning to listen to the still, small voice of the Holy Spirit in her life through the Word, prayer, and obedience. It had not been overnight, nor was it easy, but little by little, as she turned her heartache and sorrow over to the Lord, He revealed Himself to her in very real ways. God became her portion, regardless of her husband, and his choices. She had come to the point that no matter if Dan never chose to submit to the Lord, she would and would trust her Savior to meet her needs and sustain her. This is critical in our relationship to the Lord. He is not the sugar daddy in the sky, giving us everything we want, when we want it. He is our loving Heavenly Father who knows us better than we know ourselves. He knows our frailties and shortcomings.

He also sees where He is taking us, and if we realize that it is a better place than we can imagine and that the purpose of our lives is not to be happy but to be one with Him, then we can have true peace and inner joy.

Reaching this point did not mean that she did not have doubts to struggle with. She grew tired at times and emotionally drained. She dealt with loneliness and temptation, and at one point, even considered a relationship with a man who had been pursuing her. After seven years of living in an emotional desert, devoid of love and intimacy, for a moment she saw a mirage.

This man and his wife were attending our church at the time. Lori and Dan, and this man and his wife became acquainted through, of all things, a Homebuilders marriage study with several other couples. The man shared some of the struggles he and his wife were having. He seemed to pour his heart out and was sensitive. They went to counseling and were working on their marriage, his wife was very quiet and, at times, very skeptical.

Dan and Lori got together with them socially a few times and shared a few of the details of their marriage struggles, but not the true heart of what they were going through. Dan connected with the man and they became friends. Dan seemed to identify with the other man's weaknesses. The man struggled for years with infidelity and possibly pornography. The chase and conquering of women had become an addiction. He had gone to all the right counselors and seminars, and had been in accountability groups. He learned to jump through those hoops. But it wasn't real, there was no change happening from the inside out. He was a professed believer, living a lie, just like Dan.

He had gotten into another adulterous relationship and his wife had asked him to leave. He left his family, went through the motions of repentance, and again came back to church. All the while, he maintained a superficial friendship with Dan and Lori.

A few of us from church signed up to work at a youth camp that summer and he was included in the group. He and Dan spent quite a bit of time together, becoming even closer. Dan was sharing things about his feelings and the other man would seem to listen and empathize. Then he began to manipulate Dan and their friendship. Of course, Dan was using him to feel better about himself too. It was a very dysfunctional and dangerous game.

He became Dan's best friend and began calling the house for Dan when Dan wasn't home, and then would spend time talking with Lori. He was very subtle at first, all the while zeroing in on her weaknesses. Then he began crossing lines into inappropriate, intimate conversation. Talking to her as a woman, not as his friend's wife, and telling her how beautiful she was and what a fool Dan was. It did not take long to deteriorate. He began calling her frequently, and for a woman who had not felt loved or wanted by her own husband for over seven years, it felt wonderful.

However, what Dan had done did not give Lori the right to disobey God and she knew it. It only went on for a matter of weeks, but it escalated and the man wanted her to meet him somewhere. Lori knew she was in over her head. She kept this from everyone, including the First Peter Three Girls. At first, instead of cutting off the relationship entirely, she would reason with him, saying that they shouldn't be talking and it was not right. He would agree, of course. He even suggested that both Lori and he get together with Len and me for accountability. Is Satan crafty or what?

Lori knew what she had to do and it was not easy. She had crossed a line out of her weakness, and for a moment, it felt good, but then reality set in. The Bible teaches that there is pleasure in sin for a season but the ultimate penalty is not worth the price, not to mention broken fellowship with our Savior. The question for Lori again became, "is God who He says He is and do I believe He will honor His Word and meet my needs?"

She made a decision. She would not meet him anywhere and she made another phone call. Lori called me and asked if I would go to lunch with her. She wanted to talk and she was acting a little odd. Sitting in the parking lot of a local shopping center, she said she had something she wanted to tell me and then she wanted me to hold her accountable. I agreed, not having any idea what was coming.

Then she began to tell me that there was a man pursuing her and she was having trouble resisting. I knew immediately who it was and she confirmed it. She was very upset and knew that even the phone conversations she had had with him were wrong. This was real guilt; conviction from the Holy Spirit, and Lori was giving up her will and doing the right thing. I do not know how long we sat in the car with Lori pouring out her heart and crying, but it was a time of cleansing for her.

We decided that she would not talk to him under any circumstances, except to tell him never to call her again the next time they talked. She would not even initiate a call to end it. I was not sure what to tell her about how to handle it with Dan. She had not actually seen the man alone. Their inappropriate relationship was exclusively on the phone, but should she confess her sin to Dan and ask his forgiveness?

The world would tell Lori that she had done nothing that needed forgiveness, but according to God's Word, she knew she had sinned against God and her husband. Even if Dan did not deserve it, Lori's commitment was before God. We prayed about it and I agreed to tell my husband, Len, and ask him for his perspective and counsel in this situation. At first, I was leaning toward not telling Dan. What would the purpose be? However, Len, with the Holy Spirit's prompting, advised her that she tell Dan what happened. This man used Dan to get to his wife; this was about more than Lori.

It was the next day, I believe, that she told Dan what had been happening and asked for his forgiveness. It came as a shock to Dan. A friend had betrayed him. Actually, the man did to Dan what Dan had been doing to people for 30 some years—lying and deceiving, using people to get what he wanted regardless of what it did to them. He was angry. He actually said to Lori "This is me, isn't it? This is how I am."

Being on the receiving end of deception forced Dan to recognize the harsh reality of what he was. He was hurt, but not enough to repent and give up his sin. The fact that the man betrayed him was actually more upsetting to Dan than what Lori had done. Self-pity, and possibly even self-loathing, became Dan's banner. He became bitter and nursed a hatred for the man. He withdrew even further from his marriage and anyone who really loved and cared about him.

Lori shared her struggle with this temptation with the First Peter Three Girls and through prayer, support, and accountability totally cut off any contact with the man. This seemed to be another turning point for Lori in her walk with the Lord. She became more focused and sensitive to the Holy Spirit's direction in her life. She needed this in the coming months because things were soon to take a turn for the worst.

Shortly after this, Len and I sat down with Dan and Lori for a frank discussion of where they were in their marriage. My husband was serving as their deacon in the church at the time and felt a responsibility to both of them to continue to pursue them spiritually.

I remember being angry with Dan. It had been such a long battle and, after everything, there was still no change. I had to deal with my own feelings of resentment. We had all been friends for such a long time and he lied to all of us. I did not believe anything he said at this point and I was struggling with submission to my husband's wisdom in even sitting down to discuss anything with them as a couple. But, God is gracious, and His wisdom was leading Len in his spiritual role.

Len came with specific questions to ask them both and expected answers. He has a very gentle manner, which, in my opinion, made him an effective deacon. In hindsight, I believe God directed Len to ask those questions and have Dan and Lori both answer was a step in holding them accountable before

Him. If either of them lied, they would then have to own the consequences. There was no shifting blame.

Len selected several verses of scripture to read regarding the marriage commitment. After reading, he looked each of them in the eye and asked them if they had a personal relationship with Christ, "Are you saved?" Each of them answered yes. I was really struggling at this point with Dan's attitude and response. I was giving in to an ungodly attitude, and I began to make sarcastic comments. My wonderful husband, in his wisdom, told me to be quiet. Amazingly, I did. He advised me, in front of them both, that I had to take Dan's word at face value; I did not have a right to judge motive at this point. He then asked them individually if they were willing to do whatever it took to heal their marriage and fulfill their God given roles in marriage. Again, they both answered yes. Dan said he was willing to do whatever God asked him to do.

At some point after that, we spoke of our relationship as friends. I was honest with Dan about the hurt I felt and told him that it was hard for me to believe him, but I would take him at his word. He was now accountable to God for his commitment made in front of us all. We prayed with them, hugged, and then we left.

Still, in my spirit I knew Dan wasn't being truthful with himself or us but as my husband said, I had to leave it with God. It was His responsibility, there was nothing more to do but pray. Dan was still doing all the right things; there was no evidence to prove the sin that was going on in his life, but Lori knew, she lived with him.

Things went smoothly for about two weeks, which is about how long Dan would always try in his own strength to jump the hoops, and then it began all over again. I remember telling Lori, "You will know when he gets it right with God. You won't have to guess or wonder. It will be life changing for him." Lori learned not to build her hopes on Dan; he had good days and bad. In the beginning, she focused on Dan, and if he had a good day, she would think he was changing, and then when it did not last she would be hurt once again. She was past that now. At times it may seem cynical to not trust someone, but if we are fixing our gaze on Jesus and not our imperfect spouses or others, love truly does cover a multitude of sin, and God can be trusted at all times.

In the next few months, Dan began to step up the charade. He became more and more verbally critical of others, finding flaws in anyone who seemed to be genuinely walking the Christian walk. He loved gossip, and it seemed to make him feel better about himself to hear other Christian's dirty laundry.

Lori was feeling more and more as if he was sucking her into the lie he was living, and she felt convicted about the charade. Since she had not had any kind of consistent physical relationship with Dan more than several times a year, she also began to feel convicted about sharing a bed with him. In this area, most people assumed things were fine or didn't ask. It usually isn't anyone's business, but she felt strongly that pretending things were okay in the bedroom was not right because it was the area that showed the most symptoms of his sin.

Lori called me and discussed taking radical action; she felt that she should move Dan out of their room. No matter how she had begged, asked, pleaded, and reasoned with Dan, he refused a physical relationship with her. By this time, over six or seven months had passed since he had last forced himself to be intimate with her. If this was his choice then she did not want to live a lie and have it look like things were normal. It made her feel as if she was helping him in his deception.

We talked about it and prayed about it. She felt that it was what God wanted her to do, and she needed to do it. While Dan was at work, Lori moved his things to a bedroom in their basement. They had a finished basement with a bathroom, bedrooms, and living area, and many windows. It was a very pleasant atmosphere. She made his bed and hung his clothes. She did not do any of it out of anger. She just drew a significant boundary.

When he came home and found his things moved he became very angry. She had prepared for this and she stood her ground. She calmly explained that she felt this was what God wanted her to do and that God would make it clear to her when the situation changed.

Usually Dan masked his anger in passive-aggressive behavior, but as God turned up the heat on Dan, it was becoming more difficult for him to play the game; he was losing control and could not get Lori to eat that nasty food he had fixed. He told her, "I am not sleeping in the basement," and then he left. He was gone for over 24 hours and she did not know where he was or if he was coming back.

Part of the pattern of self-indulgence and sin in Dan's life showed itself in finances. He is a professional and makes a good income, but there was never enough money for them. They had a brand new home that he wanted and two car payments. Because of her past, security was a big deal to Lori, and before they married, she saved a considerable sum of money herself. Upon marrying Dan she paid off thousands of dollars in credit card debt, she paid the large down payment on the first house he wanted and she even paid for her own wedding band. Sin eventually shows up and takes its toll on every area of our lives.

Dan knew that Lori was frugal and that security was a big deal to her. That is why, 24 hours later, Dan came home driving a brand new, $28,000 truck that he wanted for years, that Lori said they could not afford. Not only was Lori living without love and affection, now he had taken away any security she had. This was a huge spiritual test for Lori.

She called me weeping. Lori is another very strong woman, not given easily to tears. As a nurse, she sees a lot of suffering and she is gentle but also very practical. She had handled many things in her life but this, after everything she had been through, seemed to break her. Dan hit her hard emotionally in the last vulnerable area for Lori.

Concerned, I immediately got off the phone and shared with Len what was going on. Len said, "Go get her." I left immediately and went to her home. She answered the door still weeping; Dan was in the background ignoring her. I didn't even go in. I just told her, "Come on, we're going for a drive." At this point, none of us could do a thing for Dan. We had already said everything there was to say. We had confronted him in love and now God would deal with him. Lori needed the support of the Body more than ever.

We drove aimlessly, and then we parked, talked, cried, and prayed. She could do this. This was another step of Lori getting out of the way and letting God work. Most people would have said, "Divorce him while you can still get something out of him. Take your kids and leave." But that is not what God had in mind.

Is God really who He says He is? Is the Bible true? We must answer these questions on a daily basis in our lives as we face whatever trials come because the answer will determine our response to those situations. If, as Christians, we do not ask ourselves these questions and answer them based upon God's

Word, then life merely happens to us with no purpose and we do not see God's hand working. Then we become complacent, hopeless, depressed, living mediocre, benign, ineffective lives, accomplishing nothing for Christ and living without His peace and joy.

Humanly Lori was hurt, but spiritually she began to soar. She regrouped and went home to face her mountain. It was time to shut up again and leave it at the altar.

Dan became angrier and more unpleasant to be around. Unable to maintain the façade as in the past, he became belligerent to her and the kids. Weekends became unbearable around him so Lori would take the kids and go for drives, take them for treats, or visit friends. Dan continued to sleep in the basement. No longer able to maintain that lie, Dan found himself alone with his sin and anger. He was angry toward God and all of us, but Lori had given it all up to God—the truck and her security, Dan, her pain, and her children living in the midst of this chaos.

For the first time Dan was truly alone, just Dan and God. There was no one standing between them and no one to blame, not his parents, or his wife, or his job, or his friends. "It is a dreadful thing to fall into the hands of the living God." (Hebrews 10:31). But after the terrible dark, there comes the glorious dawning.

Lori moved Dan to the basement and he came home with the truck in November. Needless to say, it was not a great holiday season for any of them. But God was working.

Dan did not have the money to make his first two payments on his new truck. He had leased it and halfheartedly attempted to get out of the lease to no avail. The financial pressure was mounting. Making the payments two months late left them without grocery money for that month. Still angry, the financial strain forced him to get a second job. He took a job at a local pizza place; a humbling experience for a professional, but the mess was his doing and his problem to fix.

Lori had, several years before, quit her full-time nursing job, feeling that God wanted her home with her children, especially with the problems in their marriage. She was on a casual status at the hospital and only worked a couple of days every month. She gave the money to Dan, but it was not enough either. After prayerful consideration, she decided not to give him the child support money from her first husband, feeling that it was money for her children's welfare and needs. She began using it to feed them, even if there was nothing in the house to fix that Dan had provided.

This, of course, made Dan furious, but through it all, Lori kept a level head. It was, after all, Dan's job before the Lord to provide for his family, and for Lori to usurp his position would be to sin. This is another area we, as women, tend to go astray. We think that if our husbands are not doing their jobs and fulfilling their biblical roles, then somebody has to do it, right? I have to because no one else will. Wrong. This is where trusting the Lord becomes reality.

God is big enough to care for our needs and to see that we are taken care of, even if our husbands are not following God's will. And he doesn't need our help. Again, this is a difficult concept for women to grasp. We have to learn to let go and focus on fulfilling our roles, not our husband's, or God's.

Lori refused to take control and do Dan's job for him. Dan began to bear the full brunt of the responsibility for his family and the pressure of the poor decisions he had made financially. Interestingly enough, this, and not the homosexual issue, would be part of what God used in Dan's life to get his attention.

As I have mentioned before, Dan's struggle wasn't really about homosexuality, or finances, or adultery. Those are just symptom sins. The real issue is always a deeper spiritual one; it is rebellion against God and His will for our lives. It is, as I have said before, a control issue, and this sin manifests itself in many different ways in different people.

As this personal pressure grew, the Lord also turned the heat up at church. I cannot even remember what the sermons were about during this time, all I know is that we would sit in church, listen, and wonder how anyone could resist such a strong pull of the Holy Spirit. I prayed for Dan during each service, that God would get a hold of him, break, and heal him.

Dan began to react physically after a while. He started fidgeting and he was not able to sit still, his neck and face turned beet red, but still he resisted. Finally, he started staying home for one reason or another. He was sick, had a headache, or was just too tired. This went on for a while, but the things he had committed to do in church that made him look good were the things he had to force himself to go do now. Things like playing the piano or singing in the choir, he could only miss so much without questions, which he obviously did not want to answer. It was becoming more and more difficult to maintain the façade.

Not every church does altar calls, nor do I believe that going forward is necessary to talk with God or make spiritual decisions, but Dan had said before that he did not have to go forward to get right with God. No, God does not require that of us, but if He asks us, we should be willing to do whatever He wants. Dan had basically told God he would not do that. It was pride—plain and simple. My mother used to tell me, "Don't drive your stakes because God will make you pull them up." Her mother had told her and she told me. It is wise advice. How dare we tell God what we will and will not do. When we become arrogant in our own thinking, it becomes an issue of rebellion and submission. The Bible tells us that obedience is better than sacrifice. What a difficult thing for prideful humans to learn, to rely on God's grace, not our own finite idea of what God expects. Dan was in a spiritual standoff with God and God was about to win.

It was a Sunday in late April, just before Dan and Lori's eighth wedding anniversary. The sermon was about being an authentic Christian and not pretending. It was powerful, to say the least. Len and I were sitting behind Dan and Lori and again I was praying. But, by this time, my prayers were humanly mixed with doubt. Would he ever submit to the Holy Spirit? Or would we go on like this forever?

At the end of the service, Pastor was down front extending the invitation and we were singing when Dan stepped out of the pew. I began to shake. Len began to cry. All I could see was Lori's back and I wasn't sure what she was feeling. As Dan got to the altar he spoke with Pastor then sat down and began to pray. As we stopped singing, Pastor said that Dan wanted to share with the congregation that he had been pretending for a very long time and how he wanted Jesus to be Lord of all of his life.

I could not stop shaking. As soon as the service ended Len headed down toward Dan, and Dan was practically running back toward us, bawling. Sobbing like I've never seen before, this was real. He and Len met half way, embraced, and cried together. Then as he reached the pew I was in, he grabbed me crying and saying over and over, "I'm so sorry, I'm so sorry." At that moment, I knew God had done a great thing. All my anger and frustration was no longer a struggle, it was gone instantaneously. God makes it easy to forgive the pain in light of who He is and what He has done for not just Dan, but me also. This was more than real—it was a divine change. Dan submitted to God and God freely gave Dan the grace and forgiveness He died on the cross to give. He had been waiting on Dan for 37 years.

It appeared that Dan and Lori weren't sure what to do with each other at church. Their reunion needed to be a private one. At home they would cry again and hold each other, and begin the long road back from pain and devastation to healing and restoration. "If we confess our sins, he is faithful and just and will forgive us our sins and purify us from all unrighteousness." (I John 1:9).

From that moment on, Dan was a different person, literally. I cannot even describe the changes in, not only his attitude, but also even his appearance. It is with great joy that I write this. I remember when we celebrated the year anniversary of, as Dan puts it, "When I got my head on."

It was a great milestone for all of us. Sure, Dan will struggle with the patterns in his life that were so prevalent, and, looking back over the last few years, his sinful nature challenged him at times. But he has, and will continue to, struggle through them and not be stagnate and die in them as he chooses to make Jesus the Lord of his life. I truly respect Dan's walk with the Lord. Dan has even felt God's leading toward some type of ministry work. It amazes me what God can do with a life that everyone else has given up on.

Had Lori given up on Dan and, more importantly, on God, I am sure she would have been through her second divorce with children from both marriages not having a godly father, and Dan; well I don't know where Dan would be. He would probably be missing out on the miracles and blessings God had for him. Was it worth eight years of what everyone else viewed as a living hell? For me, the answer is clear.

God is still taking each of us in the First Peter three group through trials and the daily grind of being human. Lori and Maggie's stories are the great mountain top experiences, but the other women in the group have faced struggles and victories as well while sharing life and walking together, always striving to be God's women. We are, after all, ordinary women leading ordinary lives. On the other hand, does God transform the ordinary into extraordinary for anyone who believes?

In the course of years we have been a group, we have each gone through many changes and struggles together with each of us learning from each other and supporting each other in prayer. Sex was often a topic we needed to deal with frankly. Dealing with our attitudes toward our husbands in this area and with what the Bible required of us as wives was high on our list of discussions. It was a topic in which we all had input and needed growth.

Although I do not think it is necessarily appropriate to talk about certain specifics of our intimate lives with our husbands in a group setting, I do think that women need to work through some issues in this area. We need to know that we are not dysfunctional so we don't think there is something wrong with us. We also need to know that we share a common struggle. There are some wonderful Christian books on this subject, but it is so great to have dialogue with other women about our fears and insecurities. We can learn so much from each other and, in turn, encourage one another to reach for the prize God has for us, even in this sensitive area.

Each of the First Peter Three Girls needed to lean on the rest at different times and stages of their lives and marriages.

Erica

Erica, Maggie's friend since childhood, initially struggled with taking on the work and the stress of balancing life with children while still being a godly wife and sharing intimacy with her husband. We all struggled in this area, but she took a personal inventory and other women in the group challenged her to grow in this area. This led to a wake-up call to the trouble signs in her relationship with Tom and she shared her concern for her lack of physical drive, and knew that she needed accountability in dealing with this area of her life.

After setting some personal goals to improve her attitude toward sexual intimacy with her husband, she spent a year working and saw improvement. But after hearing other women who were dealing with pornography in their marriages share some of the warning signs and situations they had been through, she began asking some general questions about men and pornography. She eventually discovered what she had been dreading, but initially did not want to admit, that it was a problem. She asked questions like, "How do you know when it is an addiction and not just an occasional thing?"

How Satan does try to deceive us. There is no such thing as occasional, willful sin. It is always a "must deal with" problem. After challenging Erica to take a hard, honest look at her life and her marriage, we encouraged her to confront Tom with boundaries. This was extremely out of character for Erica and way out of her comfort zone. Tom was initially defensive and embarrassed. He knew we all knew, but the Bible says, "Do not be deceived: God cannot be mocked. A man reaps what he sows. The one who sows to please his sinful nature, from that nature will reap destruction; the one who sows to please the Spirit, from the Spirit will reap eternal life." (Galatians 6:7-8).

We had sympathy for Tom and Erica both, but we knew this cleansing needed to happen in their lives for God to heal their marriage.

I remember my mother saying once that sometimes people need to be hurt before they can experience healing. This is so true in our lives as Christians. It is painful at times to have the Great Physician cut the cancer out of our lives, but after the surgery, we heal, and go on to live fuller, more abundant lives in Him.

It was only a matter of days after Erica confronted Tom with what she suspected and drew her boundaries before he totally surrendered it all to the Lord. They had a time of weeping and praying together on their living room floor, a time of forgiveness and healing, and, finally, intimacy they never experienced before.

It still amazes me how intricately God weaves the patterns of our lives, not leaving any thread undone. Tom went to work and through a conversation with a fellow believer that very week, found that he was not alone in his struggles, and the co-worker invited him to join a men's accountability group with him. He also corresponded with Dan a few times, sharing his weaknesses and asking for input. I get so excited when I think about how God takes care of even the littlest details of our lives when we surrender our all to Him.

Jeanie

Jeanie, Lori's friend from church, had struggled in her marriage with her husband's addiction to pornography and adultery. God also did a work of grace in the life of her husband, Tim, through a couple of different men challenging and encouraging him. He walked away from his sin; they are back in church as a family and their marriage is stronger than ever.

However, during that time Jeanie also had some tragic events happen in her family. This is an area where the First Peter Three Girls shine, as prayer partners and encouragers. Jeanie lost a young nephew in a drowning accident and she needed to be there for her sister. It devastated the family, but someone needed to be there for Jeanie as well. As most of us in the group are mothers, our hearts went out to her sister and the entire family as we shared Jeanie's grief. It was a stress on her marriage also since her sister lived out of town and she was trying to be there for her as well as still meet Tim's needs and hold her own children close.

Her brother-in-law was dealing with alcoholism, which only compounded the tragedy. Jeanie's sister and husband were not believers and through the process of grieving and healing, Jeanie was able to witness to her sister. Within a few months, she accepted God's gift of grace. These were huge answers to prayer. We are still praying for her brother-in-law, trusting God's timing.

Tim and Jeanie continue to work on their relationship, putting God first and making sure there is accountability in their marriage. It is never easy, but with God, it is always worth it.

Julia

Julia, Maggie's co-worker, also struggled with the balance of work and a family. She and Kent had three children, and he wanted her to quit her job and stay home to care for them. It's not that she didn't want to, but she struggled with letting go and trusting God to provide. Kent, being the godly man that he is, gently led and encouraged her. She finally did the hard thing and quit her job. Shortly after that, God blessed them with their fourth child. Andrew was such a blessing at that time in their lives, but shortly after he was born, the doctor was concerned that he may have a hearing loss. They ran test after test, not able to determine definitively what the damage was, but the doctors felt certain that there was something wrong. Being only a newborn, some tests would have to wait weeks or even months to determine what, if anything was wrong.

The First Peter Three Girls were on it or, I should say, on our knees about it. Regardless of what God's outcome would be, we were there for each other, supporting Julia and Kent at a time when they needed us. I also know there were many family and friends praying for Andrew. Then came the tests that would let them know the extent of the damage, and low and behold, Andrew was fine. We don't know if God healed him outright or the tests just determined there was no problem, but we do know that God was in control and watching over Andrew. For whatever reason, God took us down that path together, teaching each of us to trust Him more, even when our kids are struggling and we want so badly to fix it for them.

Mandy

Mandy, Maggie's other co-worker who joined our little group had some trying times too. Shortly after she and Bill married, he began to drink again and things began to deteriorate rapidly. God had to teach Mandy to shut up and get out of the way so He could deal with Bill. Steven and Maggie tried to spend some time with them and encourage them as a couple, but Bill continued to withdraw. They ended up moving out of town and they didn't have a computer so it was difficult to keep in touch with Mandy. We thought of her often and missed her lively personality in our group very much, but we were also prayerfully concerned that things would end badly knowing what the situation had been when they left.

Maggie attempted to contact Mandy many times but with little success. She was able to speak with her a couple of times during the next year but it was brief and Mandy just said things were fine.

A year later, Maggie received a call from Mandy. She and Bill wanted to come to town just to visit and tell her what had been happening in their lives. They knew she would understand. Apparently, things had gotten pretty bad and, at one point, Bill moved out and was staying somewhere else. Then, a friend asked them to a dramatic presentation at their church and they went. God had been dealing with Bill since his conversion, but he did not want to give up control.

God used this dramatic program to get their attention, and Bill went forward and brought Mandy with him. It was a change like Dan had experienced. They made Jesus the Lord of their lives and were so excited they wanted to let Maggie and the rest of the girls know, and it all started two years before when Maggie went out of her comfort zone and shared with Mandy.

It is awesome how God works in our lives through people who are willing to be obedient to His Word! Look at the blessings we would have all missed if Lori and Maggie had said, "No, I'm settling for the easy way out."

God works in each of our lives at different times on different things, and things are not always resolved when we think they should be. Our First Peter three group is still in the process of doing what God has called us to do, and some of us are still in the midst of less than perfect situations.

Stacy

Stacy, my friend growing up, spent over two years dealing with the pain and heartache of a daughter who was rebelling against God and rejecting her family. We all continued to pray that God would do whatever it took to get her attention. As a mother, one of the most frightening, difficult things to do is to put your child totally in the hands of God and let go, knowing they are making choices that could destroy their lives. It was a very difficult few years for Stacy and her husband as they learned how to love Jill unconditionally, yet not compromise their own beliefs. I know that it was the most painful thing Stacy had ever experienced, but I also know that she has never felt so close to the Lord and she has never had such an intimate relationship with Him. She knows more about trusting God now than at any other time in her life, and after the darkness, there also came a dawning for Stacy and her family.

Eventually they learned that Jill was pregnant. She decided to marry the father, and during the course of her pregnancy began spending time with Stacy as God gently drew her back to Himself. Healing had begun. Jill is now happily married with two children and attending church with her husband. God restored her relationship with her mother, and although Jill will bear the scars of her rebellion, God once again showed his grace and forgiveness in the midst of human failure. Stacy is also living proof of what God's grace can do in the middle of impossible heartache.

Renee and Traci

Then there is Renee and Traci. Both women, as I write this, are still in unresolved marriage situations.

Renee, my neighbor, is still living with a husband not fully committed to Christ in his walk. He is living very selfishly, which robs the whole family of a godly husband and father. But more importantly, Brian is robbing himself of the blessings that await him, when he finally chooses to take up the mantle God has chosen for him. Renee has dealt with her husband questioning whether he loved her and wanted to stay married, at least five times in the past few years. Each time she has learned more about the love of God and has learned to trust Him even when, like in both Maggie and Lori's cases, it looked more than impossible. We are still praying for Brian, and regardless of his ultimate choices, know beyond any doubt that God will bless Renee's faithfulness and commitment to Him.

Last, is Traci, my friend from junior high that God brought back into my life after many years. Traci has brought somewhat of a change to our group. Whereas the other women are still married, even if not in the best of circumstances, Traci is still alone. Kyle left her over a year ago, and after repeated attempts to encourage him to seek counseling together with her or even alone, Kyle filed divorce papers a few months ago.

We are dealing with an entirely different set of circumstances, yet still, humans are human and sin is still sin. Kyle, as I said in earlier chapters, does not have a personal relationship with Christ and wants absolutely nothing to do with God or church. As we try to encourage Traci with biblical principles, we have tried to keep the reality that God is still in control in front of us. We try to remember that if she will continue to seek His face and submit to His Word, God will honor her obedience regardless of what Kyle does. Either way God will provide for Traci as long as she remains in His will being who God wants her to be.

The difficult part is waiting, and at times, not knowing how to encourage or comfort in this particular kind of situation. Because she is married to a non-believer, the Bible is clear that Traci is free to let him go if he chooses to leave.

"But if the unbeliever leaves, let him do so. A believing man or woman is not bound in such circumstances. God has called us to live in peace. How do you know, wife, if you will save your husband? Or how do you know, husband, if you will save your wife?" (I Corinthians 7:15-16).

We believed that God could reach Traci's husband, but as verse 16 says, we didn't know what Kyle's decision would be. We had to trust God and leave it in His hands and, in the end; Kyle chose to walk away from his marriage.

We all learned together and it was a good growing experience for us all. Yet, in our humanity and doubts, we had to remind ourselves that God is always big enough to do the impossible, but only He knows what. So we waited, and prayed. We tried to encourage Traci in discerning how, according to God's Word, He would have her live during the waiting. This was not easy on any of us, but as a group, we were committed to God's purpose for bringing us together and committed to caring and loving one another through the most difficult times.

There has been many times, over the years, that we have not seen eye-to-eye, even on interpreting verses and biblical principles, or how we each have chosen to apply them in our lives. However, we have learned to practically apply God's Word and support each other in doing so, we have matured in our relationships, and learned more than just marriage principles along the way. We also learned how to lovingly confront, communicate, and forgive in the way Jesus did in the New Testament.

To be perfectly honest, at times this has been very painful. As in any intimate relationship, there was conflict and miscommunication. But early on, we set boundaries and guidelines and asked each woman to honor those guidelines out of respect for the others in the group, and to keep the commitment to God's Word the primary basis for our dialogue.

We used some key verses repeatedly that helped us in our growth together:

"As iron sharpens iron, so one man sharpens another." (Proverbs 27:17).

"Wounds from a friend can be trusted" (Proverbs 27:6a).

"Let us consider how we may spur one another on toward love and good deeds...but let us encourage one another, and all the more as you see the Day approaching." (Hebrews 10:24, 25b).

"So watch yourselves. If your brother sins, rebuke him, and if he repents, forgive him. If he sins against you seven times in a day and seven times comes back to you and says, 'I repent,' forgive him." (Luke 17:3-4).

"Therefore, confess your sins to each other and pray for each other so that you may be healed." (James 5:16).

"My brothers (sisters), if one of you should wander from the Truth and someone should bring him back, remember this: Whoever turns a sinner from the error of his way will save him from death and cover over a multitude of sins." (James 5:19-20).

"Above all, love each other deeply, because love covers over a multitude of sins." (I Peter 4:8).

A biblical foundation is crucial in our individual lives and in dealing with each other in the Body of Christ. Applying God's Word is the only way for relationships to work and become fulfilling and intimate. As we plug away in our humanness, working through so many different issues together, we have learned much about God's grace and forgiveness.

This brings me to the final member of the group, and the most difficult chapter for me to write—here goes.

You Ain't All That, Girlfriend!

The only person in the group I have not talked about is me, Marlene. Those who know me know that I always have an opinion. I am sure it is obvious by now. But my friends know never to ask my opinion out of courtesy, unless they really want to hear it because I will give it. I don't always know if that is a blessing or a curse, but it may be why I ended up being the unofficial leader of the First Peter Three Girls.

The most difficult thing for me to do is to talk about who I am. It is far easier to share that I know God put me here. But I struggle with the whys because I still, at times, wrestle with Him regarding my gifts and abilities.

I do not have a heart-wrenching, tragic story to tell about my marriage. I have been married for over 30 years, at this point, to a wonderful, godly man. I have not been through much of the tremendous pain and disillusionment that most of these women have experienced. My two adult children have personal relationships with Jesus Christ and are committed to walking with and growing in Him, and I am very proud of them. I had a wonderful childhood growing up as a pastor's daughter in a loving, Christian home, and feel very blessed for having the parents that I had. Don't get me wrong, I was not, and am not, perfect. I dealt with my own issues of adolescent rebellion and I still struggle as an adult, but I came to know Jesus Christ at an early age and have never had a time in my life where I turned away in total rebellion and felt the need to sow my wild oats. I look at the struggles that I have had in my life, but they are nothing compared to what thousands of women face every day in our society, in our neighborhoods, and in our churches.

During the most difficult times with the girls, I would often ask, "Why am I here? How can I disciple or help anyone when I cannot personally relate to many of the situations that these women face?"

"Lord, why me?"

Then, that small, still voice said, "It's not about you, Marlene!"

"Oh!"

It was arrogant of me to question God, the one who loved me enough to die for me, who created me and knew me before the foundations of the earth. I am a sinner. I am no different from any other person who was lost in sin, heading for hell, and was miraculously saved by God's wonderful grace. No matter where we come from, or what our situations are, we all stand before God unworthy without the forgiveness of His Son. God's Word applies to me just as it applies to anyone who believes in the eternal, almighty God and wants to follow Him, and the journey is not easy for any of us.

At times, I think that people who grew up in church, knowing the "right" things to say and do, are better at hiding the most insidious sins in their hearts. Following God is not just about outwardly doing, it is about inwardly being who God wants us to be, and we all have to press on toward that goal. But we never arrive. God has given each of us spiritual gifts that He expects us to use. We are not to disqualify ourselves because we think we aren't good enough or because we think we're too good. Either way, the attitude is sin.

It is our calling to glorify God, not ourselves. The focus is not me; it is God and His greatness. Yes, I struggle at times with God's call on my life, but if I do not respond to His call and if I do not use the gifts He graciously gave me, then I fail to point others to Him and I end up being the focus, which again, is sin.

Because of my background and my marriage situation, I have had many women say to me, "You just don't understand. You don't live with my husband." Or, "You've never had to live through a divorce." And they are right, I have never had to deal with some of these things, but I do know what God's Word says. I know the God who understands and Jesus, who has suffered far worse for each of us than any of us will ever be able to comprehend. A pastor does not have to experience everything each member of his congregation is going through to preach the Word and for God to use him. God knows and His Word works no matter what the circumstances or the person. It goes back to the question, is God who He says He is and is the Bible true?"

My God does miracles in my life. They may not be spectacular to the world, but they are, nonetheless, miracles because I am human and sinful, and I need His grace everyday to be who He wants me to be. If women read these stories and think they are nice, but think that the principles do not apply to all women or all situations, I have three words for them, "think again, sister!"

I can say on the authority of God's Word, not mine, that it is time to shut up, ladies, according to I Peter 3. It is something I deal with regularly. It is something that every woman I have ever met, regardless of her circumstance, has had to deal with at one point or another because we are all human and we all struggle with our sinful nature.

We cannot ever look at someone and judge his or her life just by what we think we see. We may never know the pain or struggles someone is going through. We cannot assume that someone has the perfect life and think that we are of no value to them because we cannot live up to their standards. At the same time, we cannot assume that because we have not been through what someone else has, that we cannot minister to her or challenge him according to the Word. The standard for all of us is Christ and every one of us falls short on our best day, in our own strength, without the Holy Spirit to guide and empower us. We cannot use each other as excuses not to be who God wants us to be. We cannot lie and pretend to have it all together, jumping through hoops, and somehow become self-righteous, ineffective clones of others' ideas of how a Christian's life ought to look.

I struggle with the same attitudes and sins that everyone else does, that the First Peter Three Girls all do. As a woman, I struggle with submission and what it means to have a, "gentle and quiet spirit." (1 Peter 3:4).

I need accountability and encouragement. I need the other parts of the Body of Christ to be effective in my spiritual walk and personal ministry. The faith of these women, my sisters in Christ, humbles me. I know what the truth is and I know I have to apply it in my own life, but to watch them claim the same truth in their circumstances leaves me in awe of how great my God truly is, and it spurs me on to trust Him more.

I come from a long line of fire and brimstone preachers, and it seems to me that God has quite a sense of humor to pass on a tendency to be preachy to a woman (or would that be a result of the fall?). Because the role of women in the church has caused such huge controversy in evangelical organizations, as a woman, possessing a passion to share and speak the Truth can be misunderstood. I wrestle with God over where He is taking me. I resist being considered the leader of this group, yet am compelled to press on and reach out to women as God continues to open door after door.

With every gift, because of the fall and the sin we struggle with, there seems to be a down side. We have tendencies to allow sin and Satan to distort our spiritual gifts or to use them for our own glorification. This scares me to death, but God has not given us a spirit of fear. He expects me to obey His direction in my life. In His infinite wisdom, He has given me these wonderful women to hold me accountable to His Word and to use what God has given me, not abuse it.

Maggie loves to remind me, "You ain't all that, girlfriend!" I cannot afford to take myself too seriously. None of us can. We are all in the same boat, sinners saved by grace, each with God-given gifts and abilities to press on together for the prize of the high calling in Christ Jesus.

So who is Marlene? I am just an average, normal (some would disagree) wife and mother of two who wants to be who God wants me to be. I want women to know the God that I know, the God who loves them and wants to heal their hurts and turn their mundane lives into great spiritual adventures. I want them to know the God who wants to bless their relationships with a maturity and intimacy that they can never know without Him. I want them to know the passion I feel for God and for women. I want nothing more than for them to get a glimpse of Him and His power through His Word, and to know that, no matter what, God cares and He still does miracles.

Regardless of whether we are facing tremendous difficulty at this time in our lives, or if God has blessed us with a godly, working, intimate marriage, every one of us is valuable to God and to other women in our lives.

I have a place here, but so do others. I need these women and their spiritual encouragement, guidance, and insight in my life and they need me. As Christians, we have a responsibility to one another according to God's Word, whether it is to pray, encourage, exhort, teach, or even discipline, we must be committed to each other even in our inadequacies. We need each other as women in the Body of Christ.

God has used several women in my life over the years to challenge and mentor me, long before He gave me the First Peter Three Girls. Growing up, I had a godly mother who was a living example of loving submission and discipline. Then, as a young wife, God brought Sherry into my life, who began as my ministry supervisor at Youth for Christ, but became so much more over the years. She has been, and still is, a great source of encouragement and a godly example to me, challenging me in my walk with Christ, in my marriage, and in my role as a mother. The Lord continues to bless me with godly women who make a difference in my life. My pastor's wife, Sharon, was a source of great encouragement before the Lord took her home to Glory, Diane, who is involved in full-time ministry, has challenged, and encouraged me personally and in ministry over the years. And I continue to live out the "one-anothers" from Scripture with my forever friends, Sherry and Julie, who laugh and cry with me on a regular basis. God blessed me with these women and many others, to enrich my life and sharpen me in His Word. These women were willing to get involved and invest themselves in me, and I learned much from them and their walk with the Lord. Therefore, God challenges me to do the same for others, "Teach the older women...then they can train the younger women to love their husbands and children." (Titus 2:3-4).

I hope every woman that reads this has women in their lives that they have allowed to teach, instruct, and come alongside them to encourage them in their journey as a godly woman. I hope they are involved in the lives of their sisters, investing in their growth, and sharing their gifts, knowledge, and experiences.

The Lord calls us all to teach and to learn from each other as women, which brings me to the next chapter. There are a few things that God has been working on and teaching me in my life over the past few years that I would like to share. As we say in the First Peter three group, here's my two cents.

One of the most difficult issues for us to tackle as women seems to be the s-word in marriage. No, it is not sex although, as I mentioned earlier, we have dealt with that one too. The s-word that seems to cause the most problems for women is submission. Just saying the word makes most women's skin crawl. It conjures up visions of a Neanderthal husband dragging his wife around by the hair. Today's society has so distorted the meaning of the word submission that we do not even like to say the word, much less address the biblical instruction regarding it. We are so afraid of it that we seem to skim over it as if it isn't relevant any longer. This is another lie from Satan that robs us of God's blessing.

I would like to propose a different view of the dreaded concept, what I believe to be a biblical perspective. Submission is a pro-active action, not a passive response to negative or dictatorial authority. Submission is not something husbands should enforce, but it is our willing response to God and His will for our lives. It does not mean being a doormat or allowing our husbands to control us. It is an act of my will toward God and it means surrendering completely to the Holy Spirit.

For most women submission does not come naturally. On our best day, we struggle with our sinful nature and the war between our will and God's. But because we have allowed ourselves to be convinced by society and the women's liberation movement in this country in the last three decades, we believe that we must rebel against any male authority and we have settled for carnal, superficial relationships at best. At worst, we have turned our marriages into war zones that end in the carnage of divorce where no one wins.

This flawed thinking can be subtle in its attack on our spiritual lives. Several years ago, the Lord dealt with me in an area of my life where I was not submitting to my husband's authority in my marriage. It happened just shortly before I was to speak at a women's retreat.

For about eight years, my husband worked second shift. This worked well while the kids were little and not in school. He was home the better part of the day with us and then when the kids went to bed early I would have a few hours to myself to regroup and relax. As the kids got older and were in school, it became more difficult to juggle our schedules with work and the kids and still make our marriage relationship a priority.

If left unchecked, I easily become spoiled, selfish, and undisciplined. During this time, my natural tendency led me into a comfortable routine in the evenings of enjoying "my time." I am a night person, definitely not a morning person, so I enjoyed staying up, telling myself I was waiting for Len to arrive. I was fooling myself. My time was about me. I became hooked on several television shows, which I did not like to miss, the medical drama, *E.R.*, being one of them. Of course, the shows I enjoyed came on at 10:00 p.m., which is when Len finished work. He walked in the door at about 10:30, and by then I was engrossed in some dramatic episode. I distractedly greeted him, barely giving him the time of day. He wanted to unwind and spend some time together, but I would always say, "Just wait until this is over." By the time the show ended, I would want to catch the news and by the end, Len was falling asleep, and we had not connected at all. I even got to where I moved an old black and white portable TV into our bedroom.

This went on for some time until Len finally said something. He wanted the TV out of our bedroom. I thought, "Why? This isn't fair. He is gone all evening and I am alone, with the kids in bed. I need to unwind and relax and he isn't even here so why does it matter?"

He said he felt like I did not want to spend any time with him, and that I put my shows before him and he was just an afterthought. Of course, I argued. I can be, oh so, eloquent. I had my reasons and he was being unreasonable. Of course, I cared and I did spend time with him. On and on the struggle went. I moved the TV out of the room, but a couple weeks later, I got lazy and moved it back. We argued again and Len became more and more frustrated. He even threatened to throw it out the window. "Oh, that's mature," I would taunt. It is amazing to me that I was so ridiculous and selfish. The more we argued, the more I was committed to getting my way.

Then it stopped. Len quit talking. He didn't say anything for months about it and I felt justified. I thought I wasn't doing anything wrong—just not submitting, just not respecting my husband's authority, just putting myself before my husband, just robbing myself of a more intimate relationship with the man I said I loved.

Len was hurt and worried. He felt this issue had come between us, but he no longer yelled or shared his feelings about it. I remember bringing it up at one point and he simply said, "You know how I feel," and left it at that. I had a nagging feeling that I was, perhaps, wrong. An amazing thought, but I pushed it away, ignored it.

Then my amazing, godly husband took control. With gentle, servant leadership he took action in a way that totally broke and melted my heart. I came home on this particular evening and put the kids in bed. I hadn't been to my room yet. It was dark and I could not see well, but I headed for the TV. I would just turn it on while I got ready for bed. As I reached the TV, I noticed a large piece of paper taped to the screen and the on button was not working. I thought it was unplugged. Curious, I grabbed the paper and turned on the light to read it.

As the light came on, I was shocked at what I saw. The TV was unplugged, but it had an 18-inch spike screwdriver driven through the top and into the picture tube. Breathlessly, I read this note:

I, Len Lawson, protector and guide of this home, have given every effort to negotiate with this enemy, to keep himself from this room, without success. Therefore, I have slain this vampire with a stake through the heart. He shall no longer suck the life-giving blood from this relationship.

In Humble Service to My Queen

I sat down on my bed and wept. I knew I was wrong, and I knew Len did not do this out of anger. He was totally in control when he took action, as the head of our marriage, to stop the deterioration of our relationship.

We all deal with issues in our lives and we are all called to keep pressing on toward the goal of Christ's high calling, not our own. We have lost our focus and we no longer understand what a privilege it is to be a godly woman, and no longer find joy and purpose in the responsibility of submission in marriage. We have bought the lie once again. If and when we do subject ourselves to our husband's authority, it is with negative, resentful attitudes which will undermine and destroy the very thing we as women want most in our husbands and marriages—unconditional love and security. As I have said before, we emasculate our husbands on a daily basis with our attitudes and our tongues, and then we wonder why they don't show us the love and tenderness we crave.

But remember, this is not about manipulation. Submission is not something we do to get what we want; it is about our relationship with Christ first. He was there when God first formed us in our mother's womb, He knows us best, and knows His purpose for us (Psalm 139 and Jeremiah 29:11).

I Peter 3 does not guarantee that if we submit then our husbands will do what we want or be the man we think he ought to be. But, God's Word teaches that when we submit with a godly attitude, we cease to be a stumbling block in his life and then God can use our witness to reach our husbands for His purpose, not for our purpose or pleasure. Submission honors God in both our lives and our marriage. Moreover, remember, we cannot control anyone else or make another person choose to follow God. It is that person's choice and we have no guarantee they will do what God asks. Just as we have a choice, so do our husbands. I would much rather someone be honest with me and then wait on God's direction than try to force or manipulate a response that does not come from the heart, because that choice will not last and is not real.

Do not be deceived in thinking that submission is a negative, undesirable drudgery, but also remember that it is not a manipulative ploy, either. It is a pro-active role that God gives us the privilege of fulfilling with His power. Also, do not be deceived into thinking that the quiet and gentle spirit that I Peter 3 talks about is somehow simply an outward behavior. It is not about personality because God is a God of diversity, and we each have different colorful personality traits. Some of the most controlling, defiant women I have ever known are very meek and quiet in their outward behavior, but very manipulative and deceptive in their relationships with their husbands. These women treat their husbands as objects they can control through their behavior. They seem to revere their husbands outwardly, but in reality, they have no respect for their leadership.

We must be confident in our roles, allowing our quiet and gentle spirits to come from within us. With a calm confidence and quiet grace that is from knowing the Lord is ultimately in control and that you can trust Him implicitly.

So how does submission and shutting up fit together? We'll take another look at I Peter 3.

Help! I'm Talking and I Can't Shut Up!

As women, sometimes we feel like we can't stop talking. We think that maybe if we just say something enough times or the right way our husbands (kids, co-workers, etc) will finally get it. Unfortunately, every woman I know thinks this way. It's a gender hazard.

One of the missions of our group is to help each other recognize our patterns of going on and on when we need to shut up. It is such a common problem that it has become a standing joke. Lori, at one point, wrote in an email, "Help! I'm talking and I can't shut up!"

We all laughed because we could totally relate! She recognized that she was talking herself to death and the only one getting more and more frustrated was Lori! Dan did not seem to be getting it and she was becoming more and more miserable. She was also getting in the way of God's work in Dan. Instead of Dan recognizing that God was confronting him, all he saw was Lori's nagging. She came off as critical, negative, and even self-righteous at times. Of course, that was not her intent. She just wanted Dan to understand.

"But, don't you see? How can you not understand what I'm saying?"

We have all been there and done that one. Then we come to the group frustrated and venting.

"Why can't he see it?"

"What if he never does?"

"Why? What if?"

"Shut up, girlfriend!" We will be like wallpaper, pleasant, but in the background. We will pop that corn, sit back, and watch God work. We will take our eyes off our husbands and focus on God, asking, "What is God teaching me regardless of what my husband is doing?"

We cannot let ourselves, or our girlfriends, become the foolish woman who tears down her own house. We have to be careful not to be that obstacle for our husbands, lying down in front of them, tripping them.

We have to move out of the way and just shut up! This applies to all of us, regardless of our marital circumstances. Because we are all human, even the best of marriages go through difficult times and, as Christians, we get lazy. When we begin to take God for granted, the results show up in all areas of our lives including, or I should say, especially, in our marriages.

It is very difficult to submit to God and, consequently, to our husbands as head of the home when we do not exercise the discipline of knowing when to keep quiet. When all we are doing is talking because we think that we know best what God wants our husbands to be, then we miss hearing the still small voice of God in our own lives. Again, it is the principle of being patient in the waiting room and letting the Master Mechanic work.

We tend to talk ourselves right out of the very thing we say we want. We must not settle for less than God's best for our husbands or ourselves. We can't let our desire for our husbands be driven by selfish motives or think that if he would do what we want, or be who we think he should, that that would be the best for us. The best is God's best. This is what we should seek, and we cannot see what that is, at times, until we have gone through the worst and come through on the other side changed, not just in different circumstances. We need to check our motives when we think we need to talk, or when we do shut up, or even when we submit. I cannot stress enough that this is not about manipulation. It is about being who God wants us to be. I have said many times that when God changes us it does not change our husbands, but it changes the equation, and therefore, the outcome. Two plus two equals four, until I change one of the factors. The other factor may remain the same, but the product, the outcome, is different. My husband may not change, that is between him and God, but my transformation will alter the dynamics of the relationship, and the Lord will bless my obedience. My husband has a choice, just as I do, and God is big enough to deal with him, I can only worry about me.

Our pastor has always said when talking to couples that it is far better to be second in someone's life that has put God first, than to be first in someone's life without God. It can be very scary to let go and trust God, but that is what submitting is all about. Maggie has often said that if she had gotten what she thought she wanted, when she wanted it, through all of this, she would not have ever changed. Her anger and bitterness would still be controlling her and she would not have learned how to be who God wants her to be. She would have missed the blessing, not to mention, she would certainly be divorced.

Ideally, in a growing, thriving marriage based upon biblical principles there is two-way communication. There is sharing and intimacy. But I Peter 3:1 specifically addresses, "If any of them (husbands) do not believe the Word, they may be won over without talk by the behavior of their wives." I am not saying we are never to communicate with our husbands, but the Bible gives clear direction in our lives of how to be pro-active, godly wives regardless of what our husbands choose. The best thing we can do for our husbands, whether he is walking with the Lord or choosing not to, is pray, pray, pray for him.

While we are at it, we can pray for God to show us where we need to be. Then we can be confident and content in the place God has called us to be. I also believe that if just one person in the relationship will let God get a hold of them and they will submit themselves to His will, husband or wife, miracles will happen in the individual's life, and then even the marriage. I believe this because I have seen it happen.

The I Peter 3 Girls

Ok, the girls are laughing now. They know me too well. My two cents usually turns into a dollar and then some, but there is one more thing I would like to share regarding the issue of our biblical roles in marriage.

For years, my husband, Len, has been trying to get me interested in biking. I am not a physically active person. I tell people that sweating is against my religion. He has mentioned over the years that he thought that maybe a tandem bike would be fun for the two of us. Something we could do together. A bicycle built for two—how romantic. It is a great idea, but we never got around to it, until recently.

Len and I went away for the weekend alone together to stay at a bed and breakfast near Lake Michigan. The kids were gone to a youth convention. We have always made getting away alone together a priority and this was a great chance. Len likes to plan the romantic getaways a lot of the time so he went ahead and made the arrangements.

Earlier in the week, he asked me if I would still be interested in going tandem biking with him and I cautiously agreed, although I thought he was up to something. I was right—the bed and breakfast we went to was lovely, and it had a bicycle built for two that we could use all we wanted. What a coincidence. He had seen in their advertisement that they had bicycles for use and he had specifically asked for a tandem.

Being reluctant to sweat, I was a little apprehensive about my ability to do this for any amount of time without having a coronary, but I was in for a pleasant surprise. It was a gorgeous sunny day with a cool breeze blowing in off the lake. Once we got started, five minutes did not go by and I had a revelation. This was a spiritual concept. The bicycle built for two was a perfect picture of marriage. Well, maybe not perfect, but definitely a great object lesson.

I, of course, had to share it with Len. All afternoon, everything we did and everywhere we went I could see the spiritual application in marriage. He took the front seat; his role was to lead. Even though we were both peddling, he determined what direction we took. He cautioned me if there was a bump or if we were turning. He told me when to lighten up on the peddling and when to coast. I, on the other hand, kept balance, peddled, and helped with speed and momentum. I also had a great time just looking around. I so enjoyed the day I never even considered stopping.

We biked for three hours. We went to the beach and enjoyed the view. Then we had to tackle an ominous hill. Len asked me if I wanted to get off and walk the bike up together or go back another way. I said, "No, we can do it." Half way up I thought I was going to die but kept saying, "We can do this." At the top of the hill, we stopped to enjoy the view.

It was breathtaking and we enjoyed the feeling of accomplishment together. Just past the crest of the hill, there were two benches overlooking the lake in a quaint neighborhood near an old church. Had we not attempted the hill we would have missed the cozy, intimate spot.

All day long I kept thinking, "This is what God intended." It is such a simple thing, but such a profound truth. If I had not worked with Len, if I wanted to control the bike myself, if I had not peddled with him up that hill and refused to go, not only would we have missed so much beauty, we would have more than likely fallen and wrecked the bike. We would have been frustrated with each other and there was the definite possibility that we would have gotten hurt. Each trying to do the others' job, but being in the wrong position on the bike would have been disastrous.

I don't know if it is like this for everyone, but every time we go somewhere, we forget something. Well, I forgot a camera. I was so impressed with the beauty of the day and the spiritual parallels I could see in what we were doing that I suggested we bike to a store to buy a disposable camera. The store was a considerable distance from the lake and then I wanted to bike back down to the beach, take that same hill again, and take pictures at every step so I wouldn't forget. That is the commitment God expects us to have to Him and to our marriages and the men we promised to love, honor, and obey—in sickness and in health, for richer or poorer, 'til death do us part.

It was so important to work together, to make choices about which position each of us needed to take, and whose job was what, and then how to carry out the responsibilities of that position. This is how God asks us to work together in marriage. He has given us the blueprint and assigned the roles to the best possible person and in obeying Him; He expects and plans for us to enjoy the ride even when the work is hard. It is simply an attitude of obedience to God and accepting our role in the marriage. It is what we are called and equipped to do as a woman. If we make the choice to be married then make the choice to be a godly wife. God will not let us down, even when our husbands do.

What an awesome lesson and what an awesome God that He can teach us, even through our recreation and play times in life. I will never forget that weekend and I have been after Len ever since to find us a tandem bike of our own. I might even consider sweating.

The I Peter 3 Girls

The Ultimate Makeover

God has truly blessed the "girls" who went on the journey with me, but I have a fear for the women who hear their stories. My fear is that women will, as one song says, "be stirred but not changed." That these tales of real life-change through God's grace will be perceived as a few nice anecdotes with a couple of happy endings.

That is not what this is about. And just as this is not a feel good book, the First Peter Three Girls are not just another support group or chat room. This is about real women who serve a real God who changes lives.

In our present culture we, as women, are bombarded with mixed messages from society and even the church. As I have said earlier, we have bought into the lie that says a woman's role is to compete, to succeed at all costs, and to conquer. We have been duped into giving up our gender distinctions and roles. As a result, Christian women are trying to straddle the fence between secular society and biblical principles. Women in secular society are driving themselves into the ground, chasing the brass ring they've been told is out there if they just do it all. The results are spiritually shallow women who are not ever satisfied with their lives or themselves.

The role models the media has given us in the last few decades range from obnoxious Sharon Osbourne to gorgeous Julia Roberts and from buff Jillian Michaels and to culturally influential Oprah Winfrey. Between the emphasis on physical perfection, professional success, and the spiritual journey "to live your best life" we don't know whether to work out, get a Ph.D., or just channel the aerobics instructor we were in a past life.

Women seem to be searching, as never before, for that illusive purpose and peace that brings meaning to life. At the retreat I was headed to when God dealt with me on that particular submission issue, the focus of my message for the weekend was "The Ultimate Makeover." I drew some simple parallels between our physical and spiritual lives as women.

Most women I know go through the makeover frenzy periodically. We've all been through it. We feel hormonal, emotionally drained, too fat, too skinny, bored with our clothes, bored with our hair, dissatisfied with our lives, and we need a change. We go shopping and buy new make-up or clothes then call the hairdresser and get a haircut, or perm, or a color. We join the gym or take a self-improvement class. Or we decide to go back to school for that degree we never finished. We do something, anything, to change that stagnant feeling, the feeling that our lives aren't going anywhere and that we aren't valuable because we aren't superwoman yet.

As I mentioned earlier, most women who use cosmetics understand the concept of applying makeup. We usually have a goal, or picture in our minds of what we want the end result to be. Society has given us books, magazines, and various kinds of media manuals that instruct us as to what they think the modern woman should look like. The preferred careers, the trendy clothes, the correct products to buy and how to use them and they tell us the choices "we have a right" to make. I would like to suggest that we put away all the secular manuals and go to the original, definitive book on makeovers and being successful women, the Bible. God had the original blue print and it is still the best.

Perhaps there are women who will read this and not understand the relationship The First Peter Three Girls have with Jesus Christ. Perhaps they know of Him, but do not know Him. I pray that this parallel will help them understand what "the girls" have experienced and will challenge them to look at the Ultimate Beauty Manual.

At the retreat, I talked about the three steps in a good makeover: foundation, make-up, and finishing touches. I want to share with you the principle of foundation because it is the most critical in the makeover process. The physical process first requires cleansing and treating blemishes before applying the foundation correctly. The obvious spiritual application here is, according to the Bible, we all have unsightly blemishes on our souls—sin—and without God, we have nothing with which to clean and treat them.

"For all have sinned and fall short of the Glory of God." (Romans 3:23). God has the ultimate cleanser that does not just clean the surface, but cleanses deep within the soul.

Remember application is everything, so how do we apply that cleanser? By looking in God's mirror and seeing, and then admitting that we actually have blemishes and dirt. Then we must take the cleanser from God that only He provides and allow Him to clean our lives. Again, that Ultimate Cleanser being the sacrifice of God's Son, Jesus, on the cross, whose blood takes away the sin of the world.

"You see, at just the right time, when we were still powerless, Christ died for the ungodly. Very rarely will anyone die for a righteous person, though for a good person someone might possibly dare to die. But God demonstrates his own love for us in this: While we were still sinners, Christ died for us." (Romans 5:6-8).

But, we have to accept His cleansing, knowing that we cannot do it ourselves.

"For it is by grace you have been saved, through faith—and this not from yourselves, it is the gift of God—not by works, so that no one can boast." (Ephesians 2:8-9).

God's foundation does not just cover our blemishes, it takes them away, and we then stand healed and unblemished before God. We cannot find this foundation at expensive cosmetic counters or exclusive beauty shops. It is priceless, but He gives it freely to anyone who will come to the Great Beautician. That is the final step, application, and it is crucial.

At expensive department stores, they often offer free gifts with the purchase of cosmetics, typically a pretty bag or additional make-up. With God, there is nothing to purchase, Christ paid it all, and the free bonus is eternal life for anyone who believes.

"That if you confess with your mouth, Jesus is Lord, and believe in your heart that God raised him from the dead; you will be saved, for it is with your heart that you believe and are justified, and it is with your mouth that you confess and are saved." (Romans 10:9-10).

"For everyone who calls on the name of the Lord will be saved." (Romans 10:13).

Our spiritual foundation becomes Christ, and with God, the foundation is universal. It works for everyone regardless of blemishes, or background, or baggage, and this foundation doesn't just cover our stains and blemishes, it totally removes them.

After applying the foundation, God moves on to the next steps in the makeover of our lives, the make-up and finishing touches. God uses His Holy Spirit to teach us character that adds color and definition to our lives, and then He uses our own God-given gifts, talents, and abilities to round off a completely new creation. It is the finishing touch in a fulfilled, complete, successful life as a woman of God.

For those who have not recognized the value of applying spiritual foundation, I pray that they will see it in what they have read and go to the Ultimate Beautician for the makeover that will last for eternity. For those who have accepted God's gift of salvation, I pray that they look to God's Word for the make-up and finishing touches He wants to develop in their lives.

The First Peter Three Girls are committed to helping each other in the ultimate makeover process by holding up the mirror of God's Word for each other. God uses His Word in each of our lives to develop lasting inner beauty that transcends the physical and that circumstance cannot diminish.

I have introduced some extraordinary women whom I call my sisters, and told their stories from my own vantage point in our relationships, but they have their own unique perspectives and circumstances that brought them to the First Peter Three Girls. In the remainder of this chapter, several of the girls, along with Dan, share their own thoughts and personal background that will fill in some of the gaps and they will tell, in their own words, what God has miraculously done in their lives.

Renee

There is a country song called "Looking for Love in All the Wrong Places," and for the longest time, that was a way of life for me. Wallowing so deeply in unrealized self-pity, I roamed aimlessly looking for "just the right love." My philosophy being, if he loves me enough he will do whatever it takes to please me. This was not as selfish as it sounds. I lived what I expected. I gave and gave until I had nothing left and when that still was not enough I begged, "What more can I do? What do you want me to be?"

I asked to know my shortcomings and, by golly, he told me them. After I knew them, the issue became how true they were. I had the right to defend myself, and in doing so, I would respond by listing my husband's shortcomings. Anyone can see where this was going—downhill, fast!

This pattern in my life repeated time and time again, and in the end, I was always left hurt, angry, and blaming him. Where was I to turn? The man who was supposed to be my knight, my protector, my comfort, and security was the one causing me all of my grief. Or was he?

When I met Marlene, I knew I had met a truly special friend. She invited me to her church, and included me in her circle of friends. She reintroduced me to the Father who I thought hid behind a newspaper until it was time to pass judgment, and to the Son who I thought could never repay my sins by dying for me. I was therefore avoiding my indebtedness. She reintroduced me also to the Holy Spirit, to whom my favorite saying was "la, la, la, I can't hear you," because I misunderstood His purpose.

Learning the Truth has changed my mind, my life, my heart, and, above all, my marriage. Don't get me wrong, it has not changed my husband, but it has changed how I view him and how I respond to him. It was difficult to stop passing judgment on him and turn the focus back to me, but the benefits far out-weigh the burden. When there is a conflict, I need to ask myself if I have done something to cause it. If so, I need to make the proper corrections and take responsibility for my own actions. If not, let it go. It is not mine to own. This is where faith in the fact that God is in control really shines through. I learned that I can be at peace in the middle of conflict if I just stay faithful to God's direction and purpose in my life.

I finally found the true love I had so longed for. I found Him in my Lord God. Only He can be all I need in my life. God is totally true to His Word and the only way to know this is by reading and learning His Word and then walking in His light through Jesus. Remember, if we put all of our faith in people, no matter how wonderful they are, at some point they will disappoint us. I learned to put my faith in God and I encourage everyone to give his or her heart to Him because He will never let us down.

As we all, at times, trip and fall along the path to God's Glory, we as First Peter Three Girls have made the commitment to be the helping hands to lift each other back up. As we encourage each other, we remind ourselves as well. Too often, we judge others by our own negative experiences or regrets due to poor choices made in our past that have left us cold and bitter, denying the chance for joy. God views our struggles as learning experiences for which to be grateful. Without lessons, there is no learning, and without learning, there is no growth.

Because we do tend to stray, God puts up guardrails. The effect of contact with them is directly proportional to the velocity at which we hit the rail! We can also develop a case of whiplash due to someone else's driving (which is often the case, I have found, in marriage). This still is an opportunity for learning and growth. Angry, hurtful responses never seem to produce positive results. However, as humans, we do get angry and hurt, and we react. We fall short of God's righteousness, which is why we need accountability. Our First Peter three group developed from just such a need.

Christian women dedicated, but human, sharing and supporting with in-your-face Gospel, holding each other accountable, yet loving and forgiving. The group has become a lifeline for me. Not only do we help each other stay on track in our roles as wives and our Christian walk, but we also learn to reach out to others by sharing, even each other's experiences that we may not have experienced ourselves. Though we all have different perspectives, we have one common core—our Lord Jesus Christ.

Being born again and having a group of women who care so much is truly a blessing. I know they will never let me go back to being the person I first saw looking in God's mirror. The power of prayer is unstoppable! Do so often; it works for us!

Erica

This group has meant so much to me. At first, it was just great to have contact with other women out there. Being far from family and old friends, I had felt so on my own at mothering, being a wife, and just plain living. The group provided feedback, answers, and suggestions on these things. Now, after time, the group has come to mean a whole lot more to me than that. The First Peter three group is spiritual support, in a real, honest, and caring way.

We challenge each other to pray without ceasing. We pray for each other and all the situations that come up. The group has also given me the spiritual perspective I need. We throw out our opinions and challenge each other on what scripture means and how it applies to us today as wives and moms.

Then there is the accountability. I became very grateful for this after something surfaced that my husband and I are working through. I emailed the group about a possible problem I thought my husband might have with pornography. I was almost light-hearted about explaining my concern and figured I did not have to worry. I assumed the group would think I was just overreacting. I thought I just needed to believe him when he said there was no problem. Then I heard, "Get real," "Face it," and, "Watch God move!" from the group. I got a phone call from one of the girls, and I later realized how much I needed that wake-up call. Because of the encouraging, but challenging words from the group, I was able to see the problem for what it was and how I should handle myself and respond to my husband. To make a long story short, my husband and I dealt with the problem face-to-face, and after the yelling, crying, and honesty, we gave it all to God and my husband was then free. The problem is not gone but it is now being fought with God in control and not hidden away anymore.

I am so glad that God brought me into this group. He definitely knew I needed them. I have grown and stretched, and mostly, have gotten real about what is important in my marriage based on what the Bible says and what God wants for us. I believe, as Christians, we all need this type of thing with other women. We need to be there for each other. Oh, and one more thing, we have a whole lot of fun along the way!

Jeanie

"Therefore what God has joined together, let no one separate." (Mark 10:9)

This was our unspoken rule. We were both Christians when we married. Tim was the one who had led me to Christ a few years before our marriage. We had sought counsel from our pastors. We knew we were right for each other. We loved each other.

Both of our parents were divorced. My father was an alcoholic, had committed adultery, and had remarried. Tim's father had also committed adultery and remarried. We were aware it happened, but "it" never would to us—"it" being adultery and divorce. It was not an option. Because of our rule, I really did not let the thought that we would have serious problems enter my mind. I lived in a fantasy world.

We had been married six years. We had two small children, we lived in a new city, and Tim and I both had new jobs. We lived in our first home. I was busy with involvement in ministries at church and Tim spent a lot of time at the computer. With two small children at our feet we had little time or energy for one another but I thought that was normal.

My journal entry for the fall of that year read, "Lord, please give me strength to get through these tough times. Help me to choose to love my husband. What is going on with Tim? Please change me Lord."

I remember that our Sunday school lessons were very good. We were doing a Homebuilder's Bible study and I was learning a lot. In Sunday school, I heard Maggie's story and how God was working in her marriage. Of course, God's timing is perfect. My wake-up call came the following January. I discovered Tim was involved in pornography. Then I got a clearer picture of what was happening to our marriage, but I was in shock.

Looking back, I know that God only allowed me to learn part of the problem, because that was all that I could handle at that time. God will not give me anything more than I can handle! Tim apologized and said he would do some things and I believed that everything would be fine. I went to the Bible for strength. Then I began searching for answers to the many questions I had, "Why? How could this happen to us? Our "perfect" marriage is ruined." I thought it could never be the same ever again.

In May of that year, I met Maggie who, along with Marlene, shared her testimony at a local women's Promise Reapers seminar. As I sat and listened to her speak about what she had been through, I hoped that I also could get through this.

By August, I could tell that things were not going very well with Tim. He was very withdrawn, distant, and did not want to talk about plans in our future. Then in October, I discovered the reason for his behavior. Tim was out of town with his job and I had three days to search our home. What I found shocked me enough to reach out for help. I called Lori. I knew that she was also having marriage problems. She talked and prayed with me and encouraged me to call Marlene. I spent the next few days in prayer and fasting and searching the Bible for help. Until this time, I had never felt the loving hands of God holding me. Inside I wanted to die, but I knew I couldn't. I called a few friends for prayer and I truly felt bathed in prayer.

I know that it was by God's strength alone that I got through those few days and by His peace that I was able to confront Tim when he returned home. I confronted him in calmness, yet firmly, with boundaries set. Then I left for the night to give him some time to make his decision to choose either sin or his family. As I drove, about an hour's distance away to the home of the pastor who had married us, I could feel God's presence as He directed our van down the highway. The children were screaming for their daddy and I was second-guessing if I was doing the right thing. Since Tim had just told me that he no longer loved me, nor liked being married, I was uncertain of what the future held for my family. Still, I knew that we could not continue to live with the sin. God wanted much better for us. That entire night I prayed and cried. God comforted me. I yearned to read His promises. I had never needed God so much, and He was there—holding me.

The next day Tim called and asked us to come home. He said that he couldn't promise anything and that it would never be the same, but he still wanted us to come. At first I wanted to go back to our old marriage, and then I realized that it could never be the same. And I was glad. I didn't want the lies and secrecy. He had become a stranger to me. We both wanted it different. It was very hard, I had to learn that I needed to change, not just Tim. We attended a Family Life Marriage seminar and I heard the speaker say, "Maybe God is so busy trying to work on changing you that He can't even begin to work on your husband." He was saying that to me. Wow! That hit hard. I began to realize that I had problems too and that a marriage takes two to make and two to break. Tim's addictions were his own, but I also had problems. I had to deal with control issues. I had to give these over to God, and step aside, and not be so co-dependent on Tim.

There were times when I was repulsed by being in the same bed with my husband. It was when I would think about all that had happened and how differently our marriage was turning out that it was so difficult to handle. But God showed me that I had made my marriage vows not only to Tim, but also to God. I was responsible for my own actions toward my husband. I knew that one day I would stand before our King and give my account of my behavior regardless of what he had done.

It was about this time that I joined the First Peter Three Girls. I had been talking to Lori and Marlene, but I had not joined the rest on email until this point. Maggie shared pictures that helped me visualize how I needed to react toward my husband. The group encouraged me in prayer and in words.

They reminded me, "Two steps forward and one step back."

"One day at a time, but always moving forward."

"God is in control and still working."

"God is big enough, whatever it takes!"

The following spring, in May, a sudden accident killed my five-year-old nephew. He was the same age as our oldest child. It was a very difficult time for our families. I spent a lot of time with my sister. I think it made Tim see how precious our life is and how quickly things can change. The following July, Tim attended church for the first time in nine months. He would come for special programs the children were in, but it was another year before I really felt the change.

In the meantime, God was still working on me. Lori shared with the group her struggle with another man and asked for accountability. We talked about being guardrails for each other. I was also vulnerable because of my marriage situation and felt unloved and not needed. I was lonely. I felt myself slipping into a situation similar to Lori's. Because she had shared with the group, I was alert to what was happening and quickly ended all contact with a man. God taught me that I was not beyond sin and that what I was doing was sin in God's eyes just as much as what Tim had done. I was still learning.

In May of our ninth year of marriage, three years after my journal entry, Tim and I had another heated discussion. The turning point came when he said, "You don't know me and may never trust me again, but I do—I know I'm right before God."

It was as if my heart stopped. That was the first time in our marriage that I heard and saw Tim take the lead. I knew I had to step back. I did so with joy and relief that Tim was finally right with God.

Looking back, I know that God was teaching me to trust Him more, not only with myself, but also with my husband and my family. I know that if I had learned everything that had been going on that first night three years before, I would not have handled myself according to God's will. Tim has said that if I had handled it any differently emotionally, or by threatening him, he probably would have left. He said that he went back and forth a hundred times whether to leave or stay. He didn't promise anything, but it would have to be a miracle.

God still does miracles! We are soon going to be celebrating our tenth year of marriage, and it has never been so good! I have never loved him more. God has shown us the blessing by obeying Him. When I sought advice, many people, even some Christians, said that it would be understandable for me to divorce Tim. After all, he had committed such great sins and I could just wash him away from my life. If I had taken the easy way out at the time, I would have missed the blessing that God had for us. We all would have suffered in the end. I am so thankful for my prayer partners, the First Peter Three Girls, and others, who encouraged me and upheld me in prayer to do the hard thing, the right thing. I praise God for the blessing! I praise God for teaching me to love again.

It has been a long road and I am aware that it still will be. I am thankful for what I have learned. Romans 8:28, "And we know that in all things God works for the good of those who love him, who have been called according to his purpose," means much more to me now. Many people say that something good will come out of every situation that God brings our way. I never wanted to believe it, but now I have seen it!

Julia

I became involved with the First Peter Three Girls at a turning point in my life. Before my husband and I were married and up until after we had our second child, we were once a week churchgoers, attending a local Catholic church. Then a friend invited my husband to a Promise Keepers Conference and our lives have never been the same. He made a personal commitment to Jesus Christ and after sharing his newfound faith with me; I too committed my life to Jesus. Kent began to deepen his relationship with the Lord and has become the strong spiritual leader that he is called to be.

I, however, had come to a point in my life where I needed to make some decisions. I had just become pregnant with our fourth child and we were debating whether I should quit my part-time job and become a full-time, stay-at-home mom. Up until this point, nothing had seriously challenged our faith. We were about to be tested. I had always worked at least two or three days a week since shortly after I had my first child, and the prospect of being home with four children ranging in age from newborn to seven was quite overwhelming to me.

The two older children were becoming quite active in extracurricular activities and I was having a difficult time getting them to and from everything on time, even working only a few days a week. I felt torn between work and my need to be there for my children. I felt I was cheating both and running myself ragged. I tend to be a perfectionist and I was feeling my performance in both areas was definitely less than perfect and it really bothered me. Kent had been traveling quite a bit with his job so the responsibility fell mostly to me. He could see and feel the tension that this stress was causing and he initially suggested that I quit. At first, I was totally against the idea, thinking that my patience could not bear being home with the children all day long and that they were much better off with a sitter. In addition, we just moved into a new home in a nice subdivision and we certainly could not afford for me to quit working, but God had a different plan in mind for me and He began to soften my heart.

It was during this time that I began to develop a closer relationship with my friend, Maggie, at work. We had talked about our faith, our families, and many other things. She introduced me to the First Peter Three Girls and asked me if I would like to join them. These women immediately accepted me into their group and I began to communicate all of the issues I was dealing with in my life. They prayed for me and encouraged me to seek God's will and to follow His calling. Since my husband was eager for me to be at home, they encouraged me to trust God in this area and follow my husband's wishes. They are so good to me. They gave me Scripture to refer to and they guided me. They spoke from the heart and from their own experiences. To make this long story short, I did finally decide to quit my job about a month before the baby was born. Just before my last day on the job, my wonderful husband arranged for my family and friends to send me cards and letters of encouragement to support me in my decision. I will never forget my last day of work. I returned home after a very emotional day, Kent sat me on the couch and presented me with all of the cards, letters, and email messages that he had collected. I sat on there and cried tears of joy and relief, as I had finally committed to our decision. Each one of my First Peter three sisters had sent something and it meant the world to me.

During the next few months, God confirmed this decision in our lives. We were to face another test after the birth of Andrew, our son. Almost immediately after we brought him home from the hospital we noticed that he did not appear to startle or respond to noise like a newborn should. And, believe me, there were many people and noises in our home to be startled by with the six of us. We took him in for testing at five weeks, and the results confirmed our worst fears. He appeared to have a significant loss of hearing. After the initial shock and grief, we got on our knees and sent out prayer requests to family, friends, and, of course, my First Peter three sisters. They were mothers. They could relate to what I was feeling.

It would be months before they could run tests that would determine the extent of the hearing loss, and those months were some of the longest of my life. Andrew was almost five months old when that test took place. The First Peter Three Girls prayed and fasted along with us on that scary but glorious day as we sat in amazement in the technician's office as she performed the tests and Andrew scored perfectly in all ranges and pitches. It was a miracle, and we witnessed it right before our eyes. Thanks to the wonderful grace of God and the faithful prayers of our friends and family, Andrew could hear!

I have not been faced with the major challenges that most of the women in our group have been faced with, nor was I brought up in a Christ-centered, Bible-teaching home, but I am learning and growing in my walk daily. I hope to be able to give back to these women and others as much as they have given to me. I have acquired the official title of cheerleader of the group and it seems to fit. I pray that I can be that and much more to them in the future.

Although I do not regret my decision to be a full-time, stay-at-home mom, I still struggle with it at times. I have had my own issues to deal with, such as the time and energy to have an intimate relationship with my husband, and then the emotional strain in losing my mother to cancer. But in each of these situations, these women have been there for me to listen, to give me sound biblical guidance, support, and encourage me, and most of all, to pray for me. They are all a true blessing to me and I look forward to continuing to grow and learn together as we strive to be all God has called us to be.

Stacy

I have really learned so much from this whole situation with our prodigal daughter. It has been a real growing process for both Greg and I, and we could not have made it without having Jesus Christ as our personal Savior. We still have our bad days, but I think the biggest lesson has been to trust God and really put our faith in Him, knowing that He knows the big picture and we don't. We like to think we are in control, but when these things come into our lives, we realize that God wants control and wants us to relinquish our control over to Him. I praise God everyday for my special First Peter sisters in the Lord; they have stood by me with so much encouragement through the past couple of years. It has been a real blessing to have them in my life and to know that they will say it like it is and not just pacify me. I love every one of them and each one brings a different perspective and gift to this group. Praise God that they have been there in my time of need!

Maggie

I cannot even begin to describe how important this support system has been to me. It was so awesome having other Christian women pointing me to

Christ and holding me up when I felt like going limp. It has been my lifeline. So many times, in my devastation I felt very alone. I had absolutely no support from anyone regarding working on my marriage. My husband loved another woman. People told me, "There's a point in a bad marriage where there's no turning back. Why would you still want to be married to him?" I often wondered, "Am I so insecure that I will cling to my husband and stay married when he doesn't want me?"

Do not buy Satan's lies. Love is a choice. Not to love our spouses is a sin. God has already proven he is bigger than sin. As Marlene described, I am, by nature, a very strong woman. I will not be a doormat for anyone. But through seeking God's will I determined that if God wanted me to be what seemed like a "doormat" then so be it. Weak women do not stay in bad marriages and seek to live God's will. Strong women do!

"Jesus looked at them and said, 'With man this is impossible, but with God all things are possible'." (Matthew 19:26).

Divorce is not God's plan for us. God can do anything and change anything. He can trade beauty for ashes and strength for fear. We can become the very creatures God created us to be by obeying His Word. My God is the God of the impossible. It has been such a blessing for me to see how far my husband and I have come. We are truly different people. We don't have the marriage we had years ago. I know in my heart I would have truly missed God's blessing had I left my marriage for someone who I thought could love me. I am truly thankful for this group of women who God used to help restore my life and guide me in the right direction. I am also grateful for my forgiving, loving God, who cared enough about me to get my attention in order to have a much fuller, richer relationship with Him.

Lori

The First Peter Three Girls have been a great support and encouragement to me, discipling me in my growing relationship with Jesus. It was a big job. The group shared the burden. Someone from the group is usually able to respond when a concern is voiced and we can take turns as God leads us—sharing the emotional and time-consuming burden of listening to, empathizing with, giving advice, and praying for each other.

When women are discouraged we need help. This society does not offer a lot of truly biblical help. Even Christian counselors gave us an out for divorce (except for one counselor, Dave—thanks Dave). Christian women do not need an out. We need to hear that God does miracles today. We need to vent our feelings and then have wiser women tell us to hang on to God's Word and pray. We need to believe that God is big enough to do anything and that God cares enough to do it. We need friends who will confront us with our flaws and help us to change. We need accountability. We need patience. We need to love and trust God whatever the outcome. We need support to walk through our troubles because Jesus died on a cross for us. He loved us enough to die for us. Yes, it is painful, but not as painful as what Jesus did for each of us.

We all need friends to quote us Scripture like, "Jesus looked at them and said, 'With man this is impossible, but with God all things are possible'." (Matthew 19:26).

And, "You are the God who performs miracles; you display your power among the peoples." (Psalm 77:14).

I did not journal during the bad times. I just wanted to survive day by day and not ever look back. I am more inclined to write now about what God has done. It is a visible miracle.

The change in Dan has been truly unbelievable. I was so skeptical in the beginning. I didn't want to hope for real change and then be hurt again. But this change was real. The people who really know him saw it. I saw it, the kids saw it, and our close friends saw it. God changed Dan's heart. Dan only had to surrender his will to God's will.

Dan started to talk about a joy he felt that he never had before. He looked happy. He started to get frustrated with superficial relationships. He wanted honesty and meaning in his relationships. God brought a childhood friend back into Dan's life, and it quickly came out that they shared more than they ever knew—an addiction to pornography. God put Dan into a position to disciple this other man and it has been a huge growing experience for him.

Dan cared more than ever about his relationship with me and with the kids. I saw the kids starting to love their dad more and enjoy his company. Dan started to see the frustration that he had put us through with his deceptions. He longed for more meaning and honesty in his relationship with his parents and sibling. He strove to care about others more and to show it. When he would slip back into his pattern of procrastination and laziness, he would more quickly see it and correct the problem.

Then, a few months ago, Dan said that he felt God calling him to apply for a ministry position out of town. I could see that God was speaking to Dan. And, more importantly, I saw that Dan was listening. The job is unrelated to what his degree is in and it would require a major change in our lives, but Dan quickly acted on what he felt God was leading him to do and obeyed God. We have not heard anything as of yet, but we are waiting to see how God is going to work this situation out in our lives. We are willing to obey and go where God sends us.

I love my First Peter three sisters. They have been here with me and witnessed this awesome miracle. They are the kind of friends who point me in the direction of God. They lift me up and encourage me. God has truly blessed me with this group of women.

A Few Words from Dan

Marlene asked me to write something for *The First Peter Three Girls* book, and after some thought and prayer, I agreed. I would write something. But what? What did I really want to say? What did God want me to say? I wanted to read the book first, and then I might know what to say. She was afraid to let me read it. She thought that I might get angry. As I was reading what she had written, I wanted to say, "Wait a minute! That's not me!" Then I would think, "Yes, that was me." Each time I read something she had written about me, I wanted to say, "Yeah, but what about this?" or, "What about that?" She was writing from her perspective and as I was reading, I wanted to give the reasons for the way I acted. For instance, I wanted to tell about when I was young, probably eight years old, when an older neighbor boy approached me and did things that were inappropriate and the time in sixth grade, when another boy my age approached me and we did things that were inappropriate. I also wanted to talk about my family. We were a good, loving family from all appearances, a Christian home, but no one talked about important stuff. We only talked about how things should look on the outside.

I could blame many things, many people, and I did. I even blamed God. Because God could remove these thoughts and feelings if He wanted to, and believe me, I asked Him many times. But I had taken some things that happened to me and nurtured them for years and years. I thought getting married would solve my problems, but that only compounded them. I felt relieved when I finally spilled my story, but I didn't want to change. I said I did, and believe me; I tried to change, but only in my own strength. It did not work. I would go through the motions, and then I would let my feelings get in the way. I wouldn't feel like doing what I needed to do for real change.

I guess what I am trying to say, is that we all have a choice. Sometimes it seems clearer than at other times. The choice is whether to submit our will to God. See, this is what Marlene is talking about in this book. These women made a conscious choice to submit their will, their desires, their hopes, and dreams to God. Lori got lots of counsel. Some was wise, and most of it was well intended, but not very godly. From a pastor's wife to "Christian" counselors, they told her to take the kids and leave me. After all, she did have biblical grounds for divorce, but there was this First Peter three group who encouraged her when she needed it. Sometimes she would tell me what they said in an effort to get me to change, but I would say, "They only know your half of the story." I was sure she was tainting the picture in her favor. If they only knew the whole story, they would see it my way, I thought. Everyone else had it all wrong, at least from my perspective. From hindsight, I praise God that Lori had the First Peter Three Girls for support. I think without them, she would have taken the other advice and left me long ago.

I put Lori through a lot of pain, much more than I may ever know or understand. I can see that Lori is a woman who wants to please God, truly a woman after God's heart. God truly worked a miracle in our lives and he took care of the rest of the story. In my life it was not about homosexuality, it was about doing what was right in God's eyes, and in submitting my will to His.

My life was all about deceit and making people think that everything was okay when it really wasn't. I went to church, sang in the choir, was on the praise team, played the piano, etc. I thought I was fooling everyone, but I was the one who was the fool. Then, one day, God asked me to walk down the aisle at church and tell everyone that I was pretending. How could I do that? I had done such a great job of pretending, what would people think? There was my pride again causing me to stumble.

It really is a simple choice, to submit our will to God's. The choice is simple, but the work and the cost seem, at times, too much to bear. However, since I have submitted my life and my will to God, I have known joy that I did not know before.

Do I struggle with old feelings and habits? Absolutely, yes. But God is bigger than all of my struggles and he has done, and continues to do, a good work in me as long as I submit to Him. Philippians 1:6 says, "Being confident of this, that he who began a good work in you will carry it on to completion until the day of Christ Jesus." I really believe this, and I think verse five tells us that it really is a choice. Verse 5 says, "because of your partnership in the gospel from the first day until now." If we don't submit our wills in partnership with God, then we are the losers. We can question in all of our circumstances, where is God? But He never leaves us. God created us for fellowship with Him, but He loved us enough to give us a choice, a free will.

I will close with a verse that is special to me. "Neither death nor life, neither angels nor demons, neither the present nor the future, nor any powers, neither height nor depth, not anything else in all creation, will be able to separate us from the love of God that is in Christ Jesus our Lord." (Romans 5:38).

God is so awesome. I get overwhelmed reading what Dan and the girls shared. Based on the evidence, let me answer the questions that I have asked repeatedly.

Yes, God is who He says He is and, yes, His Word is true! Believe it, accept it, live it! Then reap the unspeakable blessings of an intimate relationship with the God who loves us and wants to heal our hurts. The First Peter Three Girls have lived this and we want to share it with the world. We also want to challenge all women to find out what it means to be a First Peter Three Girl, according to God's Word, and then to pass on the legacy.

Let's boil this down. What does it mean to be a First Peter Three Girl?

As a child of God, I must be committed to obeying God's Word and applying it in my daily walk. I must carry out all of my roles "as unto the Lord." As a wife, I must be committed to my husband and the role that God has called me to fulfill. As a mother, my first responsibility is discipling my children. They are a gift, and God commands me to "bring them up in the training and instruction of the Lord." (Ephesians 6:4). But, as a believer, He also calls me to go and make disciples in my world. Even more specifically, as a woman, I am told that I am to participate in the Body of Christ by also teaching and instructing younger women and sisters in Christ in the ways of the Lord, teaching and challenging them to a high calling in Christ Jesus. We are to spur each other on, to move forward together.

The First Peter three concept is not a new one; it is a biblical one. God is the author and commands us to participate in the Body of Christ; using the gifts he has divinely blessed us with in our relationships. We have simply put a name to our particular method and organized practical application. The message is, as it has always been, that God saves and transforms lives. We are committed to sharing that and encouraging each other to press on toward the goal.

As we have shared our individual lives and testimonies with other women, and as I have had the opportunity to speak to women's groups, women have many questions about the group. They want to know how we organize it and if there are guidelines that we follow. As we began to add to our accountability group, one by one, we realized we needed to set some boundaries in place to keep us focused and on track. Here are the guidelines we set and the commitments we made to one another.

- WE AGREE: The purpose of the First Peter Three Girls is for the developing of intimate female relationships that encourage and edify us as sisters in Christ. We will hold each other personally accountable in our daily walk with Jesus.
- We will keep information shared within the group or share only to spouses (if appropriate). This ensures each persons' privacy, gives that person freedom to share sensitive issues and gives the others freedom to respond in an uplifting, biblical manner.
- We are each free to vent but not bash. This includes personal attacks directed toward spouses, friends, co-workers, relatives, and each other. Freedom to vent enables us to be real and honest with our feelings and yet vulnerable to each other so we can confront in love, encourage, admonish, forgive, work through, and grow together.
- We will limit the number of individuals in the group because we will have a greater impact on each other in a smaller, more intimate setting. A limited number also ensures the privacy of each woman.
- We will hold each other up in prayer and fast together.
- We will limit our prayer requests to individuals in the group or immediate family, and to situations that relate to each person in a way that we can keep track of and understand as we get to know that person.
- We will work on memorization of scripture. "I have hidden your word in my heart that I might not sin against you." (Psalm 119:11).
- We will fulfill our commitment to one another when the other women need us. We all have times when we are needier or busier than others, and we need to be able to count on each other as our time and families allow.

This is the basic framework for our group. We are committed to being guardrails for each other. When we get off track, the guardrails tell us that the path we are on is dangerous. Sometimes we actually run into a guardrail and the collision mangles both of us a little, but it is worth it to save a life.

As for the practical application of the First Peter three principles, we are always learning and we spend much time praying, always directing our attention to our own wrong patterns in our marriages. We often deal with the submission issue and what it means, and does not mean, in each of our unique situations. We have spent time trying to pinpoint our tendencies toward manipulation and control. We have dealt with identifying false guilt and enabling patterns. We have even tackled the sex issue and our tendency toward not meeting the needs of our spouses in this area. And, of course, one of the critical issues we each face continually is when to shut up and let our husbands take responsibility for their own choices and behavior. Only with the power of the Holy Spirit and prayer are we able to effectively deal with and change these patterns in our lives as women. God is loving and gracious enough to give us each other to sharpen, challenge, and come alongside for support.

We have also had great times of fellowship together in person. We initially saw a need to get together face-to-face after our group had grown and so many of us had not actually met. After our first meeting, we had such a great time talking and sharing together; we decided to make it a priority every few months. Sometimes it is just for a few hours over dinner, or at one of the girl's houses sitting in a hot tub laughing and just being women. Occasionally we try to all meet at a hotel for an overnighter, which turns into an all-night sharing and prayer session. It's not always easy since some of us live out of state, but we see it as important in making the concept work. The times we gather face-to-face are necessary for connecting as believers. It helps to remove the impersonal distance and misunderstandings that sometimes accompany email communication. It also establishes better communication and accountability once we have met in person. We are not just words on a computer screen, we are human beings and it is so easy to lose sight of that in this age of technology when, with the click of the delete button, we can erase a person's identity from our screen. Talking face-to-face strengthens our commitment to each other and deepens our relationships. Besides, it can be just plain old fun—a time when the joy of the Lord rings loudly and it certainly does within our group.

A WORD OF CAUTION

We are all, as believers, sinners saved by grace and we are all at different places in our walk with the Lord. To become involved in such a commitment means to be willing to have patience with each other. This may mean disagreements and dealing with a weaker sister at times. We all come with baggage of some sort and different issues, but we humbly press on together.

"Not that I have already obtained all this, or have already been made perfect, but I press on to take hold of that for which Christ Jesus took hold of me. Brothers (sisters) I do not consider myself yet to have taken hold of it. But one thing I do: forgetting what is behind and straining toward what is ahead, I press on toward the goal to win the prize for which God has called me heavenward in Christ Jesus." (Philippians 3:12-14).

The bottom line should always be God's Word and pressing on toward maturity together. Dig, dig, and dig in the Word. Hold each other to it. Encourage each other with it. Love each other as it says to. For an accountability group to really be effective it should include at least one or more spiritually mature Christian women who can be trusted to keep things on track and can rightly divide God's Word and direct others to it. There may be times when we need a mediator to help group members who disagree. To work through these times is to mature and grow in grace and the knowledge of our Lord. I have wept at times over and with these women. I have hurt for them. I have been on my face before God with them. Through it all God has grown me along with my sisters. As we develop godly disciplines, we begin to get a glimpse of how big our God really is.

We also need to caution ourselves, as women, to make sure that any group or organization, even church responsibility, does not take away from our responsibilities and relationships at home. We cannot afford to live vicariously through the lives of others or with a sense of self-importance as if we are the only ones who can help individuals. The relationships we cultivate in an accountability group should enhance our roles as wives, and not become a substitute or priority over our God-given roles and relationships in our families. We need to be building up each other's marriages, not spending time husband-bashing or fill all our time being there for, and helping, others that our own families suffer. God has solutions, not band-aids, and if it doesn't play out in our lives at home, we cannot be a true help to others. I cannot ask anyone to obey God's Word if I am not willing to do so myself.

I pray that I walk before my own daughters and granddaughters in a manner worthy of the calling of mother. I want to pass on the First Peter three legacy. I want to teach them what it is to walk in wisdom, to exercise discernment, and to reach out to their friends and sisters in Christ. I want them to know what the Bible means by a "quiet and gentle spirit." I want them to feel the passion for a God who is passionate about them. I pray that, as they grow and mature, God brings into their lives other girls and women committed to being God's women; to hold them up in prayer and challenge them in their walk. And I pray that God gives me the wisdom as a mother and grandmother to raise the next generation of First Peter three girls who will honor their God and husbands and will pass the legacy on to their own daughters some day. I pray that, no matter what circumstances they find themselves in, each woman that reads this book finds the redeeming message of God's love, grace, and hope that He brought to these women. I challenge each one to become a First Peter Three Girl and then pass the legacy on.

ABOUT THE AUTHOR

Marlene Lawson is a trained Biblical Counselor, certified Christian Life Coach, and author of *The I Peter 3 Girls* book and small group Bible study. With over 32 years of ministry experience, Marlene is a regular speaker at women's events. She has opened for national speakers and authors like Liz Curtis Higgs, Angela Thomas, and Kim Bolton. As a wife of almost 35 years, mom, and grandma, Marlene brings her own candid viewpoint and brand of humor to her writings and speaking presentations. Her ministry is to challenge, encourage, and assist women in becoming all that Christ created and saved them to be.

I am a middle aged, hormonal woman with the gift of gab. I am a communicator by nature, which means I have difficulty shutting up sometimes. Well, often, which seems to be the struggle of my life, along with losing weight and getting fit—whatever that means. Fit is something my clothes do not do well, but I can certainly throw a good one. My passion to reach women is God-given, whether I like it or not. At times, I have not appreciated this calling and have had many discussions with God on the matter, but I am learning to accept that He knows best and to surrender to the inevitable. My belief in Truth will always remain anchored in God's Holy Word. I want all women to join me on the journey of discovering the exciting adventure He has for us riding the rollercoaster of life! So ladies, grab a cup of coffee, or a mocha frappe—which is my drug of choice, and we'll chat!

Contact Marlene:
www.marlenelawson.org
www.nowwheresmypenny.wordpress.com
marlene.lawson@aol.com
Marlene Lawson Author

I Peter 3 Girls Book Club Discussion Questions

1. Having read chapters one and two, what is your initial, gut-level reaction to Lori's situation?
2. Do you think that there may have been warning signs that everyone ignored? What do you think our responsibility is to warn or share concerns with our family members or close friends when you notice red flags in a relationship?
3. From a Christian perspective, what do think Lori should do in response to Dan's confession?
4. Putting yourself in her place, or if a friend found herself in a similar spot, what do you think you would do or say to a friend?
5. Having read through chapter five, what do you think most people's reaction would be to Lori and Maggie's situations?
6. What do you think the role of the church or Christian friends should be in situations like this?
7. Where does the Bible come in and how do you think it affects the circumstances for Dan and Lori and Maggie and Steven?
8. What is an example of the "lie" that Lori and Maggie had to face in their situations?
9. What Scriptural Truth, shared in the book, would be the most difficult for you to accept if you were in their situations?
10. How do you think the "lies" in our culture affect Christian's perspective of marriage?
11. What is your reaction to these women's interpretation of I Peter 3, specifically the directive to "shut up?" Do you think that the verses in I Peter 3 apply to today's culture and marriages?
12. What is your reaction to the concept of submission in the Bible? How would you apply this concept today in our culture?
13. What do you think submission looks like in a relationship where the husband is either not a Christian or is a professed Christian, but is not living it?
14. Give an example of when it might be good not to shut up. Do you remember a situation in the book when the women did not shut up?
15. What is the difference between venting and bashing?

16. How did the friends that Maggie, Lori, and the others turn to make a difference in how they responded to their husbands and circumstances?
17. How did the "what ifs" affect the women in the book and how they responded to their husbands and the issues they faced?
18. Describe what kinds of fears the women in the book faced.
19. Give an example of fears or "what ifs" in your own life that affect how you respond to relationships or that keep you from doing what you know God wants you to do.
20. In the book, Lori was struggling with false guilt. Give an example of where she drew a healthy boundary.
21. What did Maggie have to face that had contributed to the problems in her marriage?
22. What is the difference between false guilt and conviction? Give an example of both.
23. How did boundaries, or the lack of them, contribute to the difficulties in the marriages in the book?
24. What would a healthy or unhealthy boundary look like in a difficult marriage situation?
25. Which of the situations in the book would be the most difficult for you to forgive and why?
26. What does the Bible say is the first step to forgiveness and is it necessary?
27. Do you really believe forgiveness is possible for the people in the book? In your own life?
28. What have you learned about yourself through the stories of the women in this book?
29. What Truth in God's Word has become more real to you or has convicted you as you read their stories?
30. Do you think you could become a First Peter Three Girl and are you willing to be accountable to godly women and be there for others? Why or why not?

I Peter 3 Girls Personal Bible Study

This is a very basic Bible study. It's not fancy and does not include profound sermons or new answers. God's Word is very straightforward and simple. It has not changed since He inspired its writing a couple of thousand years ago. The difficult and complicated part is our response to it. Whether we believe it and take God at His word, surrendering to Him when it doesn't make sense to us in a chaotic, sin-driven world. The challenge is to get alone with God and His Word and examine our own lives, circumstances, and perspective in light of what He has to say. Will it affect what we do? Does it really matter? Does it have anything to do with who I am and what I am going through? I pray that you discover God's answer for you in whatever struggles you are facing as you walk alongside the First Peter Three Girls in this book and dig in to God's Word.

Each of the eight sections is designed to cover a week and contains corresponding chapters to read in this book, along with a Food for Thought statement to consider as you read the assigned verses, and a Memory Truth to meditate on each week. The few verses listed just tap the surface of what God has to say to us on these subjects, but will give you a glimpse of who He is and how much He loves you. At the end of each section is a Prayer, Praise, and Progress Journal for you to write down your thoughts, struggles, and what you are learning about yourself and your God on your journey with Him. Each section ends with a place to write the most significant revelation you discovered during that week's study.

Let's get started on your adventure to becoming God's First Peter Three Girl!

Week One: Understanding Who God Is

Read through chapter two, Where Do We Go From Here?

Food for Thought:

Is the Bible true and is God really who Scripture says He is? In light of the Scriptures you study this week contemplate on who God is, what He's done, and what He has promised you. Do these questions and answers change how you view your current circumstances or your role in your relationships?

"For I know the plans I have for you, declares the Lord, plans to prosper you and not to harm you, plans to give you hope and a future."

Memory Truth- Jeremiah 29:11

Read one daily Scripture selection each day for six days and, keeping in mind the Food for Thought statement and your own circumstances, use the section below to jot down your thoughts, struggles, and responses to what you read. This exercise is about you and God so let the Holy Spirit speak to you this week!

❶ Genesis 1:26 - 2:25   ❷ Job 37 & 38
❸ Psalms 18   ❹ John 10: 7-18 & 27-30
❺ John 14:6-21   ❻ Hebrews 4:14-16

✍Week One Prayer, Praise & Progress Journal

1 _____

_____

_____

_____

2 _____

_____

_____

_____

3 _____

_____

_____

_____

4 _____

_____

_____

5 _____

_____

_____

6 _____

_____

_____

This week's "light bulb" revelation: _____

_____

_____

_____

_____

_____

WEEK TWO: WHAT DO YOU REALLY BELIEVE?

Read through chapter five, Who Me?

Food for Thought:
You do what you do because of what you believe. Do you believe God has a plan for you in the circumstances you are in? What does that say about your beliefs and how you are responding to your present circumstances? This week ask the Lord to reveal areas where you may have doubt about Him and His Word

"His divine power has given us everything we need for life and godliness through our knowledge of him who called us by his own glory and goodness."
Memory Truth- 2 Peter 1:3

Read one daily Scripture selection each day for six days and, keeping in mind the Food for Thought statement and your own circumstances, use the section below to jot down your thoughts, struggles, and responses to what you read. This exercise is about you and God so let the Holy Spirit speak to you.

❶ 1Samuel 16:7 & Hebrews 4:12-16   ❷ Philippians 4
❸ Romans 12   ❹ 1 Peter 2:19-25
❺ Matthew 12:34b & Romans 15:4-5   ❻ Hebrews 3:6-15

✍Week Two Prayer, Praise & Progress Journal

1 _____

_____

_____

_____

2 _____

_____

_____

_____

3 _____

_____

_____

_____

4 _____
_____
_____
_____

5 _____
_____
_____
_____

6 _____
_____
_____
_____

This week's "light bulb" revelation: _____
_____
_____
_____
_____
_____

WEEK THREE: FACT OR FEELING? IDENTIFYING THE LIE

Read through chapter eight, I Quit!

Food for Thought:
Feeling follows action; action follows belief; belief follows thought process. What you think about, meditate on, and tell yourself is what you will end up believing and that is what will determine your actions. Be aware this week of your thought patterns that contradict the Scripture you study and make a concentrated effort to change them by focusing on the Truth.

"If any of you lacks wisdom, he should ask God, who gives generously to all without finding fault, and it will be given to him. But when he asks, he must believe and not doubt, because he who doubts is like a wave of the sea, blown and tossed by the wind."

Memory Truth- James 1:5-6

Read one daily Scripture selection each day for six days and, keeping in mind the Food for Thought statement and your own circumstances, use the section below to jot down your thoughts, struggles, and responses to what you read. This exercise is about you and God so let the Holy Spirit speak to you.

❶ Psalms 4   ❷ Psalms 16:7-8 & 9:9-10
❸ Philippians 4:4-9   ❹ 2 Corinthians 4:7-9 & John 16:33
❺ 1Peter 1:3-7 & 13-15   ❻ James 1:2-8 & 12-16

✎Week Three Prayer, Praise & Progress Journal

1 _____

_____

_____

_____

2 _____

_____

_____

_____

3 _____

_____

_____

_____

4 _____

_____

_____

_____

5 _____

_____

_____

_____

6 _____

_____

_____

_____

<u>This week's "light bulb" revelation:</u> _____

_____

_____

_____

_____

_____

Week Four: Why & When To Shut Up!

Read through chapter 11, Erica and Jeanie

Food for Thought:
Submission is not a passive reaction, but rather a proactive act of the will in response to God's promises. When we get out of God's way and follow His Word in difficult situations it allows Him to work in us and perform miracles in our lives. That is when we learn to trust Him and we experience growth. It is easier to "shut up" when we get our eyes off of others and onto the God who loves us and blesses our obedience.

"Whatever you do, work at it with all your heart, as working for the Lord, not for men, since you know that you will receive an inheritance from the Lord as a reward. It is the Lord Christ you are serving."

Memory Truth- Colossians 3:23-24

Read one daily Scripture selection each day for six days and, keeping in mind the Food for Thought statement and your own circumstances, use the section below to jot down your thoughts, struggles, and responses to what you read. This exercise is about you and God so let the Holy Spirit speak to you.

❶ Proverbs 14:1 & 17:1, 14, 19   ❷ I Peter 3:1-2 & 9-11
❸ James 1   ❹ James 3:3-15
❺ Proverbs 21:9, 26:4, 5, 15:1   ❻ Psalms 4:4 & Proverbs 10:19

✍Week Four Prayer, Praise & Progress Journal

1 _____

_____

_____

_____

2 _____

_____

_____

_____

3 _____

_____

_____

_____

4 _____

_____

_____

_____

5 _____

_____

_____

_____

6 _____

_____

_____

_____

This week's "light bulb" revelation: _____

_____

_____

_____

_____

_____

Read through chapter 14, Traci

Food for Thought:
The enemy uses fear (or "what ifs") to paralyze us and distract us from the Truth, which leads to ineffective, impotent faith and mediocrity. This week, ask the Lord to reveal to you where you have been paralyzed by fear and show you where you need to step out and act in faith based on the Scriptures we have studied.

"I took you from the ends of the earth, from its farthest corners I called you. I said, 'You are my servant'; I have chosen you and have not rejected you. So do not fear, for I am with you; do not be dismayed, for I am your God. I will strengthen you and help you; I will uphold you with my righteous right hand."

Memory Truth: Isaiah 41:9-10

Read one daily Scripture selection each day for six days and, keeping in mind the Food for Thought statement and your own circumstances, use the section below to jot down your thoughts, struggles, and responses to what you read. This exercise is about you and God so let the Holy Spirit speak to you.

❶ 1 Samuel 12:14-16, 24 ❷ Psalms 33:18-22 & 3:3
❸ 1John 4:18 & 1Timothy 1:7 ❹ Luke 12:1-31
❺ 1Peter 3:13-17 ❻ Romans 8:14-18 & John 10:14-18

✐Week Five Prayer, Praise & Progress Journal

1 _____

_____

_____

_____

2 _____

_____

_____

_____

3 _____

_____

_____

_____

4 _____

_____

_____

_____

5 _____

_____

_____

_____

6 _____

_____

_____

_____

This week's "light bulb" revelation: _____

_____

_____

_____

_____

_____

Week 6: Dealing With Guilt & Setting Boundaries

Read through chapter 16, The Dawning

Food for Thought:
We experience false guilt when we believe lies of Satan that we are responsible for another person's sin or that God has not truly forgiven or accepted us. However, true conviction from the Holy Spirit through Scripture challenges us to take responsibility for our choices and surrender to Christ. That repentance brings true healing and lasting freedom. This week consider the relationship between guilt and drawing boundaries.

Memory Truth: Romans 8:1-2

"Therefore, there is now no condemnation for those who are in Christ Jesus, because through Christ Jesus the law of the Spirit of life set me free from the law of sin and death."

As you read the Word this week keep in mind the Food for Thought statement and during the first three days consider what the verses say about feelings of guilt or condemnation, what we should or shouldn't feel guilty about, and what our response should be to genuine conviction.

❶ Hebrews 9:14-15 & 10:15-22　　❷ 1 Thessalonians 4:7-8 & James 4:17
❸ Romans 2:1-7 2 - Corinthians 7:8-10 - Psalms 139:23-24 - Galatians 6:3-5

The last three days think about what the verses are saying about our independence from others, their control over us, our dependence on God, and how that should influence boundaries in our relationships. Remember, this exercise is about you and God so let Him speak to you.

❹ Matthew 14:22-23 & 4:1-11　　❺ Romans 14:8-12
❻ 1 Corinthians 4:2-5 - Ephesians 5:6-10

✍Week Six Prayer, Praise & Progress Journal

1 _____

_____

_____

_____

2 _____

_____

_____

_____

3 _____

_____

_____

_____

4 _____

_____

_____

_____

5 _____

_____

_____

_____

6 _____

_____

_____

_____

This week's "light bulb" revelation: _____

_____

_____

_____

_____

_____

WEEK 7: FORGIVENESS: MISSION POSSIBLE

Read through chapter 18, You Ain't All That, Girlfriend!

Food for Thought:
The Bible teaches, and even secular studies show, that holding on to bitterness, hurt, and anger only hurts us and can consume our lives. Bitterness is like a cancer that permeates every relationship and if left unchecked, will destroy us. Why give Satan that kind of power when you can be free of that bondage when you forgive others as Christ has forgiven you? Forgiveness and true healing are possible. It is your choice to surrender your hurt, betrayal, and anger toward a person or situation to Christ!

"And do not grieve the Holy Spirit of God, with whom you were sealed for the day of redemption. Get rid of all bitterness, rage and anger, brawling and slander, along with every form of malice. Be kind and compassionate to one another, forgiving each other, just as in Christ God forgave you."

Memory Truth: Ephesians 4:30-32

Read one daily Scripture selection each day for six days and, keeping in mind the Food for Thought statement and your own circumstances, use the section below to jot down your thoughts, struggles, and responses to what you read. This exercise is about you and God so let the Holy Spirit speak to you.

❶ Ephesians 1:7-8 & 4:20-32   ❷ Colossians 1:10-23 & 3:13-15
❸ Matthew 6:14-15 & 18:21-35   ❹ I John 1:9 & Hebrews 12:14-15
❺ Acts 10:43 & Luke 6:36-38   ❻ Romans 12:17-21

✍Week Seven Prayer, Praise & Progress Journal

1 _____

_____

_____

_____

2 _____

_____

_____

_____

3 _____
_____
_____
_____

4 _____
_____
_____
_____

5 _____
_____
_____
_____

6 _____
_____
_____
_____

This week's "light bulb" revelation: _____
_____
_____
_____
_____
_____

WEEK 8: THRIVING VERSES SURVIVING

Finish the book

Food for Thought:
Jesus wants to restore our lives, taking the faded hues, worn threads, and knotted tassels of everyday wear in a sinful world and re-make them into the passion, purpose, and vibrant colors of this adventure He has called us to live in Him.

The analogy of a beautiful tapestry is so like our lives when we turn them over to Christ, the Master Weaver. He takes jumbled layers of disconnected threads and weaves them into a work of art. At first, it looks like a tangled mess, but the finished piece is breathtaking. His handiwork in our lives makes sense of the disorder we create. Let the Lord craft you into His masterpiece by surrendering your will, your life, your circumstances, and your loved ones to Him!

"For I know the plans I have for you," declares the LORD, "plans to prosper you and not to harm you, plans to give you hope and a future."

Memory Truth: Jeremiah 29:11

As you read through this final week's verses prayerfully consider these continuing challenges:
- ♦ Get to know the God who loves you and created you
- ♦ Tell yourself the Truth of God's Word—"think on these things" (Philippians 4:8)
- ♦ Act on the Truth of God's Word in your life—let the Scripture direct your actions
- ♦ Trust God with your fears and false guilt—give them to Him daily
- ♦ Forgive and keep forgiving—"as Christ has forgiven you" (Colossians 3:13)
- ♦ Shut up—ask for wisdom to know when to be silent and when to speak
- ♦ Embrace the Truth and live the adventure—Thrive! Don't just survive!

❶ John 10:10 & James 1:2-5, 12   ❷ 1 Peter 1:6-9 & 5:6-11
❸ Philippians 4 & 2:12-15   ❹ Psalms 18
❺ Proverbs 3:5-6 & 4:4-14   ❻ Psalms 3

✍Week Eight Prayer, Praise & Progress Journal

1 _____

_____

_____

_____

2 _____

_____

_____

_____

3 _____

_____

_____

_____

4 _____

_____

_____

_____

5 _____

_____

_____

_____

6 _____

_____

_____

_____

This week's "light bulb" revelation: _____

_____

_____

_____

_____

To order a more in-depth small group study and leader's guide please visit:

www.marlenelawson.org

NOTES

NOTES

NOTES

NOTES